DAVID

David

The Divided Heart

DAVID WOLPE

Yale

UNIVERSITY
PRESS

New Haven and London

Frontispiece: *David and Goliath*, engraving by Gustave Doré, 1866.

Quotations from 1 and 2 Samuel are taken from *The David Story: A Translation with Commentary of 1 and 2 Samuel*, by Robert Alter. Copyright © 1999 by Robert Alter. Used by permission of W. W. Norton & Company, Inc.

Yale University Press books may be purchased in quantity for educational, business, or promotional use. For information, please e-mail sales.press@yale.edu (U.S. office) or sales@yaleup.co.uk (U.K. office).

Set in Janson type by Integrated Publishing Solutions, Grand Rapids, Michigan.
Printed in the United States of America.

Library of Congress Cataloging-in-Publication Data

Wolpe, David.
David : the divided heart / David Wolpe.
p.   cm.—(Jewish lives.)
Includes bibliographical references and index.
ISBN 978-0-300-18878-3 (cloth : alk. paper)   1. David, King of Israel.   I. Title.
BS580.D3W65 2014
222'.4092—dc23
2014006335

A catalogue record for this book is available from the British Library.

This paper meets the requirements of ANSI/NISO Z39.48-1992
(Permanence of Paper).

10 9 8 7 6 5 4 3 2 1

To Steve, Paul, and Danny,
brothers and companions through life

CONTENTS

_____

In MY HIGH SCHOOL, parents of graduating seniors were assigned a page in the yearbook to write a message to their children. Decades ago, right before graduation, I opened up my high school yearbook to see what my parents had written to me on their page. In the name of the whole family, my father submitted the following:

> And David sang many songs.
> The people listened and heard.
> They sang his songs and were comforted.
> They loved David and thanked
> the Lord for him.
> He became a beloved gift unto all the people.

Deeply touched, I went right to the book of Samuel to find the source. I soon realized my father had selected, arranged, and added to create the message. It was also then that I became fascinated by my namesake. Aware of David's story, I had never really wondered—what was his power to comfort and why was he beloved? The songs he sang echoed through the ages and Israel was blessed with their spirit. So who was this man?

Upon being invited by Yale University Press to write on an eminent Jewish figure, for me the choice was easy and obvious. I had since learned that David was no simple shepherd and songster. This king of Israel was the Bible's most complex character. His life was entangled with war, women, and offspring who both betray and succeed him. He won battles and feigned madness, founded a city and served an enemy ruler, slayed a giant and fled from his own child.

But my father's essential message remained. The name David means beloved, and no character in the Bible is as loved as David. The first time in the Bible that a woman is said to love a man is when Michal loves David. Her brother Jonathan loves David. The people of Israel love David. Even Saul, who bears a murderous rage toward David, is said first to love him. Finally, we are told that David is a man after God's own heart.

So a little less than forty years (a good biblical number) after my curiosity was first stirred about the biblical echoes of my name, I have distilled a lifetime of wondering into this short book about a remarkable man.

I am now much older than when my father, of blessed memory, wrote those words in my yearbook. Life has made David seem more real—more human. No longer persuaded or enchanted by the purism of youth, I have come to expect contradictions in every human soul, and to defend the stubborn integrity of the divided heart.

INTRODUCTION

Who is David and who is the son of Jesse?
1 Samuel 25:10

WE WISH our heroes to be attractively flawed: brave but heedless, good but confused, wise yet inexplicably sad. A minor crack in character makes the vessel seem that much more precious. Still, while acknowledging the complexity behind the clarity of Lincoln, or the darkness that lurked beneath Churchill's inspired eloquence, we fix on the uplift and ignore the downdrafts.

David confounds such simplicities. Other ancient figures have stories, powerful ones; but they are fragments of character, marked by tendentiousness and heavy symbolism. David is the first person in history whose tale is complete and vital, laced with passions, savagery, hesitation, betrayal, charisma, faith, family—the rich canvas of a large life. He is capable of great acts, expressions of lasting piety, and of startling cruelty. David's failings are not slight or endearing. Whitman famously said of himself that he contained multitudes. Long before Whitman, the Bible's premier poet had a soul so large that thousands of years of interpretation have not exhausted its landmarks and byways.

From this distance we cannot know what is a literal recounting and what is invention or distortion. The character of David convinces, along with its shocks and incongruities. Surviving rebellions, fraternizing with the enemy, committing public adultery and proxy murder, David dies peacefully in bed. Scarred, still roiled by revenge untaken, having lived a hard life, he remains essentially unharmed. We read of his uneasy relationships with wives, children, his warriors, and the people. His story is like the Gestalt experiment: You can choose to see David as hero or knave. His enemies keep disappearing, but he disclaims any part in their death. He sustains enough loyalty to remain king but also endures rebellion, even from within his own family. The explanation of traditional piety is simple and elegant: God is with him. The modern reader suspects that while trusting in God, David is a man careful to secure himself a little earthly insurance nonetheless.

Novelists take advantage of the story's ambiguity. Stefan Heym's *King David Report* depicts a court historian trying to tell the truth about David but under constant pressure to exaggerate his righteousness. (One character says to the historian: "If you know as much as I think you know, Ethan, I think you know too much.") The novelist, who lived part of his life in communist East Germany, understood what it was to try to tell stories with shadows about those in power. A powerful state versus the truth is the theme of Heym's tale, and he uses ancient Israel to indict the modern regime.

Historian Pieter Geyl wrote a book called *Napoleon: For and*

Against, chronicling the opposing views of historians on Napoleon. A reader of the commentators and scholars on David could compile a similar book. One portrays him as a paragon of faith who fell but once, another as a Machiavellian villain who cannily rose to rule. Each has hold of a piece of what makes David so compelling. The drive to see David's character as perfectly consistent betrays a blinkered view of human nature. David contains more than any single explanation can embrace. He is, in the words of historian Baruch Halpern, "the first human being in world literature."

Why would this man, king of a small, warring land, be chosen by great religious traditions to give birth to the Messiah? Why must the Messiah come through the Davidic line? No less remarkable than the man himself is what religious tradition has done with him. David, fissured and flawed, is held up as the exemplar who is forerunner of the world's redeemer. Surely there is a less ambiguous ancestor, although we would search in vain for a more intriguing man.

David's story is told in the Bible in very loose chronological order. It is crammed with incidents and characters. To recount the tale meticulously would require a longer book, and might not leave us any wiser about the character of David. So in the pages following I have walked through David's life and written about each of the roles that define him—the Young David, David as Lover/Husband/Fugitive/King/Sinner/Father/Caretaker/Messianic forebear—and have included other roles as poet, musician, and warrior. Inevitably these categories will flow into one another, but in the end, cutting across slices of the story to build a picture of this man, we will have a rounded portrait. Then perhaps we will be better able to answer the question: Why, of all the characters in history, does David hold such an exalted place?

Here is a drama full of deeds heroic and base, a story of faith in God coupled with an equal pursuit of power and military might. It is also a story of the power of women. Women, as we shall see, repeatedly push the hinge of the narrative in the direction it needs to go. The presence of women is complemented by the absence of miracle. God is invoked so often that even some skilled readers fail to notice that, with the murky exception of raising Samuel from the dead, there is not a single supernatural miracle in the entire story of David, the longest continuous narrative about a human being in the entire Hebrew Bible. At times it seems that when David needs a miracle, God finds a woman to enact it in an earthly manner. Benefiting from this divine/distaff bounty is a man whose relationship with women is the most detailed and complex in the Tanach, as the tripartite Hebrew Bible—Torah (Pentateuch, Ta), Nevi'im (Prophets, Na), and K'tuvim (Writings, Ch)—is traditionally known.

So versatile and enduring is David in our culture that rare is the week that passes without some public allusion to his life. Every sex scandal involving prominent men is sure to evoke comparisons with David and Bathsheba. Successions in power allude to David and Saul. Unequal struggles are summarized with the battle of David and Goliath. Few symbols fulfill so many functions: If you reach for an underdog, if you seek a precedent for the abuse of power, if you look for an ancient model of friendship or (perhaps) same sex love, if you want a monarch who is also a bard, if you want to suggest a kingship that will never end, and so very much more—David is your man. He is a character whose reputation is as ramified, as remarkable, and as enduring as his story.

As Amos Oz writes in *The Same Sea* of an ancient king so seemingly modern: "with his leaping and dancing and his one-night stands/It would have been more fitting for him to reign in Tel Aviv." We need to understand David better because we use his life to comprehend our own.

This brief study attempts to get at the heart of a character with the aid of commentators ancient and modern. The effort to understand David is never-ending; there is no tiring of his life or legacy. To this day at almost every celebration, Jews sing, "David, King of Israel, alive, alive and everlasting."

The two major controversies that swirl about David as a historical character are the sources of his story and the size of his kingdom. There was once a considerable debate over whether David indeed existed. To this day it remains an uncomfortable fact that nothing unequivocal has been found that can be traced to his hand or identified with his rule. Nonetheless, relatively recent discoveries of two inscriptions have more or less put the question of his existence to rest. A stele (that is, an inscribed monument) from Tel Dan in Israel contains the words "The house of David." Although the stele is dated from a little less than two hundred years after David, it seems improbable, to say the least, that two hundred years later a king (probably Hazael of Aram-Damascus, though it is uncertain) would identify himself as having defeated an adversary from the house of a man who never existed. The discovery at Tel Dan led to the announcement of the same expression on the famed Mesha stele (also known as the Moabite stone), which was roughly contemporary with the Tel Dan inscription. There is another possible, perhaps likely, mention of David's name in the list of places claimed as conquered by the Egyptian king Shoshenq a hundred years earlier than the Mesha stele, the "highlands of David." While none of these is dispositive, taken together they make it extremely unlikely that David is a fiction.

Although it was once believed that David ruled over a large kingdom, modern archeologists are convinced that his sway was far more modest. No contemporary chronicles have been discovered that mention David or Solomon, as would be expected in the case of a substantial kingdom. David was fortunate to flourish at a time when the two dominant powers in the area, Egypt and Assyria, were relatively dormant. The space probably allowed for no more than a small principality in a backwater land.

There are robust, ongoing arguments about the authenticity of a structure currently under excavation that is claimed to be David's palace. A well-planned and fortified city has been found some twenty miles southwest of Jerusalem, on the summit of a hill that borders the Elah valley, in modern-day Khirbet Qeiyafa. Even those who argue it is not David's palace, however, agree that it indicates a major settlement from the time of David. Additionally, there are archeological sites with possible links to the stories of David, though none of them is certain. One of the difficulties of archeology in Israel is that it is impossible to escape a political valence to each spadeful. Nonetheless, one can securely say that David existed, probably presiding over less grand a land than we had imagined, and that his story cannot yet be corroborated in any particular.

But what a story. Since so much of the book of Samuel, which tells us of David, reads like an apologia—a claim that David was not involved in the elimination of the house of his predecessor, King Saul, or complicit in other nefarious deeds—the text gains credibility by its very unease. If you are inventing out of whole cloth, why assume you have to cover up bad deeds for a hero who did not exist? David might have been guilty or innocent, but the debate even in ancient times was evidently a lively one.

Who wrote the book of Samuel that tells the story of David? (It was once one book but for convenience divided into two, 1 Samuel and 2 Samuel. Scrolls are unwieldy). Virtually all modern scholars of the Bible discern at least two major strands, and perhaps more: the story of David's rise and the struggle for succession. Some divide the primary documents into an earlier and later contribution. Competing stories jostle one another for narrative or theological priority. Sometimes this leads to evident contradictions—it is hard to figure out the sequence of David's anointing, defeat of Goliath, and entry into Saul's house, for example. But the greatest contradictions, the most fascinating and enduring, are in David's character, and here the story reminds us not of conflicting sources but of the fissures inside this enigmatic man.

The bulk of 1 and 2 Samuel was probably written not long after David's death—perhaps during Solomon's time—and certainly while the Israelites still lived in Judah, which they did for four hundred years after David. (The Southern Kingdom—that is, Judah—was destroyed in 587 BCE by the Babylonians. David lived some four hundred years before, around 1000 BCE.) In an age when oral traditions were the lifeblood of the society, that means that David's story was handed down, orally and in bits of writing, for an indeterminate time after David was no more. We cannot say with any certainty how long the text was added to or tinkered with. Perhaps several versions competed with one another for prominence and left their mark. The result is an intricate, fuguelike work.

The writers (let us assume plurality) of the book of Samuel were artists of genius. The later biblical book of Chronicles retells the story, but censors objectionable parts and makes it more pious. In other words, Chronicles is Samuel made boring. The characters in Samuel are vivid, powerful, individual; even small sketches like Paltiel weeping for his lost wife Michal as she returns to David, commander Joab sending a messenger back to David assuring him that Uriah has been murdered, the dramatic denouement of Absalom's rebellion—these moments, described below, stay etched in the reader's memory as the highest expression of narrative. David has been claimed by scholars as the first great work of history, the first biography really worthy of the name in a modern sense. Whoever these initial artists were, they have rarely been equaled. They left us an account of a warrior-poet-hero wily as Odysseus and tortured as Lear, yet as faithful as the "shepherd of Israel" (Ps. 78). They gave us David.

DAVID

1

Young David

OUR FIRST glimpse of David is his absence. Saul, the king
of Israel, has fallen into disfavor, and Samuel, the high priest,
sets off in search of a new king. Samuel goes to the house of
"Jesse the Bethlehemite" and asks him to present his children.
Jesse marches the first, Eliab, a tall, handsome, strapping figure
of a man, before the distinguished visitor. Samuel is convinced
that he has met the new king. God's voice intervenes: "Look
not to his appearance and to his lofty stature, for I have cast
him aside. For not as man sees does God see. Man sees with the
eyes and the Lord sees with [or 'into'] the heart" (1 Sam. 16:7).
Jesse subsequently marches the rest of his seven sons before
Samuel. Each in turn is rejected by God. Seven is the perfect
number; the eighth is an afterthought.

Right at the beginning we find the ambiguity that will trail
through David's story. Although in Samuel he is identified as
the eighth son, in Chronicles, David is called the seventh son.

The seventh is perfect in biblical numbering. So is David perfect and the shining star or an afterthought who is not worthy of being introduced? Samuel throughout offers spin-images—David as seven or eight; good or bad; innocent or schemer; hero or knave. Tell the truth, wrote the poet, but tell it slant. David's is the Bible's great slanted story.

The stage is set. All seven sons have been set aside. Samuel asks, "Are you sure you have no more sons?" Yes, replies Jesse, there is the youngest out back, tending the sheep. He is summoned; young, handsome, ruddy cheeked. We have met David.

Later, when the question of fathers and sons plays an enormous role in David's life, our minds naturally turn back to this first moment, when his father scarcely even thought of him. David was absent; not present in the scene, or in his father's mind. It took Samuel's question to bring him forth. The man who grows unseen by his father will struggle all his life with children.

The identification of David as a shepherd in this first scene recalls a biblical pattern: Jacob was a shepherd, as was Moses. The Rabbis, seizing on this, say explicitly, "When God wishes to choose a leader, God looks to see how he tends sheep" (Ex. R. 3:48–49). In other words, will this person be good to the powerless and the lost? Can he be a caretaker? In identifying David as a shepherd the Tanach is telling us: Here is someone with a steady hand and a compassionate heart. The subsequent tale complicates that image but never quite erases it.

In these early days we meet a David who is easy to love. His introduction is his anointing. There is no suspense about this young man's destiny. David will be king. And God dictates the drama—God, who is rarely direct in the story of David, speaks unambiguously about the divine choice. Samuel, confused at first about the worthiness of Eliab, receives his instruction.

How does Samuel arrive at Jesse's house? Saul, the first king of Israel, has disobeyed God by leaving Agag, king of the

Amalekites, alive. Whatever Saul's motivation (humane or self-interested), it finally convinces Samuel, the priest who objected to the idea of kingship to begin with, that Saul must go. Under divine instruction Samuel is dispatched to the house of Jesse to choose a new king.

While we do not yet know that David will be a man of guile in his greatness, there is a hint in God's initial instruction to Samuel. When Samuel quite reasonably protests that King Saul will seek to kill him if he finds out he is on his way to anoint the new king, God instructs Samuel to lie: "Take a heifer with you and say, 'I have come to sacrifice to the Lord'" (1, 16:2). A white lie, to be sure. A lie to preserve a life. Still, it is worth noting that David is anointed in a cloud of mild deception. Does he at this moment learn to adopt the self-protective shading of the truth from the prophet who gives him his start?

Samuel pours the oil on David, and "The spirit of the Lord gripped David from that day onward" (1, 16:13). We are about to read a story of a king, beleaguered, at times desperate, who is nonetheless astonishingly lucky. Here is the Bible's explanation. God's spirit has gripped him. He can betray, he can sin and stumble, but he cannot fail.

What awaits David, newly crowned? We are witness to three separate introductions. The chronology is more interesting as a character study than as a literal ordering of narrative. The next incident in David's life is that he is sent to Saul, the king, who suffers from bouts of melancholy.

Half of David's story, the ascent, consists of his gradual displacement of the king of Israel. Saul has been a frequent subject of long-distance psychoanalysis. He is a man with an unprecedented task as Israel's first king, subject to manic mood swings and beset by an unsympathetic high priest in Samuel and a resolute and demanding God. Moreover, Saul is a paranoid with real enemies. Saul is tall and imposing, but his physique betrays him. His external size hides his timidity. Early in his kingship he is already hiding, a frightened man unfit for rule.

The first encounter between Saul and David is poignant or chilling. Saul's attendants, noting his dark mood, suggest finding a lad who is skilled in the lyre, an ancient musical instrument, to play and coax the melancholy king back to fitness. The initial recommendation is a powerful foreshadowing. Saul's attendant says he knows of a young man, "skilled in playing, a valiant fellow, a warrior, prudent in speech, a good looking man, and the Lord is with him" (1, 16:18). With that formidable list of virtues, Saul is convinced. He seems to know of David, for he sends messengers to Jesse asking him to send his son "who is with the flock." It reinforces our understanding of David as shepherd but also establishes the peculiar intimacy that will grow between the fading king and the rising one.

The most widely accepted meaning of the name David is "beloved." The first person who is said to love David is not his father or mother but Saul: "And David came and stood in Saul's presence, and Saul loved him greatly" (1, 16:21). Later, David will win the loyalty of Saul's family, marrying his daughter and befriending his son. Saul, however, will seek to kill David, not once but several times. David will finally succeed him. In this earliest encounter Saul sees what Israel will see: the charisma of that young man summoned to cheer him. Saul will never entirely lose that initial love, and the stark split in his feelings about David is one of the many forces that tears him asunder; Saul will always love the one he hates and fears. The man who evokes this mixed feeling in Saul will summon equally strong reactions in many who cross his path, as he does in those who read his story centuries later. From his first moments on the biblical stage David is marked both by the passions he feels and those he evokes.

After David is summoned to the house to play, his music helps soothe Saul, temporarily at least. "David would take up the lyre and play, and Saul would find relief, and it would be well with him, and the evil spirit would turn away from him" (1 16:23). Our first introduction to David is as the shepherd, musician, and attendant, an artist and an aide. There is a sweetness in the portrait of the early David, often belied by the man he will become.

The battle with Goliath is the best known of the David stories. It has an enduring appeal to the belittled and downtrodden. Phillis Wheatley, America's first published African American poet, chose "Goliath of Gath" as a subject for one of her works, published in 1773:

> Thus David spoke; Goliath heard and came
> To meet the hero in the field of fame.
> Ah! fatal meeting to thy troops and thee,
> But thou wast deaf to the divine decree.

As often happens, the memory of the story is less nuanced than the original telling. There is a powerful undercurrent present to the careful reader. Painter and historian Giorgio Vasari tells of young Leonardo in the workshop of the master Andrea del Verrocchio. Leonardo contributed an angel to Verrocchio's painting that was so masterful that the teacher laid down his brush and resolved never to paint again. The announcement of a prodigy is wonderful and painful in equal measure. David, like the young Leonardo, is gifted beyond anything Israel has seen. Saul, however, will not lay down his crown. The struggle to supplant him will be long, rocky, and painful.

The outline of the story is simple: Goliath, the towering Philistine champion, issues a challenge to Israel. No one will step forward to fight him until David, young and unimposing, challenges him, trades taunts, topples him with a stone from his sling, and decapitates the felled giant with his own sword.

But this oak of a story has seeds that will grow in directions we might not expect.

Before taking on Goliath, David was sent by his father to take food to his brothers who were already at the front. While there, David hears from the Israelite men milling about, both of Goliath's challenge and of the possibility of reward for anyone who can defeat him.

For the first time David speaks. It is a biblical commonplace that a character's first words are defining: "What will be done for the man who strikes down yonder Philistine and takes away insult from Israel? For who is this uncircumcised Philistine that he should insult the battle lines of the living God?" (1, 17:26).

Here is the characteristic Davidic combination of idealism and self-interest, mixed with stunning self-assurance. David wishes to know what is in it for him. He also feels the national and even theological affront of Goliath's impudence. Underlying both is the certainty that, should he choose to fight, he will win. Unlike other Jewish notables such as Moses, Jonah, or Jeremiah, David has no unease about his suitability and readiness for his mission.

His older brother Eliab, dismissive of David and upset that he has left the sheep behind, accuses him of voyeurism, a wish only to see the battle. David answers in the manner of younger brothers throughout the ages, "What have I done now? It was only talk" (1, 17:29). The following verse is unobtrusive but definitive: "And he turned away from him." David turns from Eliab, no longer a child, striking out on an independent destiny.

The troops hear David's words and report them to Saul. Saul naturally brushes aside the possibility that this stripling can fell a giant. David insists, boasting that he has killed both lions and bears in his years as a shepherd, but never mentioning his skill with a slingshot. In a piquant touch, the Rabbis further tell us that David's clothes are made from the wool of the sheep that he saved from the claws of beasts, in thanks to God for his deliverance. The rabbinic commentators of the Midrash suggest that David's triumph over wild beasts foretold the possibility of future greatness. Perhaps the tradition assumed he must have received the hint from his own experience, since God has not told David he must kill Goliath. David just *knows*.

Saul has been left with no other volunteers; he fits the young man with his armor. In a scene heavy (in all senses) with symbolism, David is unable to maneuver in Saul's armor and strips it off. Garments will play a role throughout the story: when Saul pursues David, David will, unbeknownst to the older man, cut off a piece of Saul's coat so that he can later prove to Saul that he was close enough to kill him. When Samuel ultimately strips Saul of the kingship, Saul will grab at a piece of Samuel's cloak, which will tear. The Hebrew word for coat, "beged," is related to the Hebrew word for betrayal, "boged." Clothes unmake the man.

Saul seems not to know who the young David is, even though David has already been attending him and playing music in his house. This could be a product of inattention, of Saul's depression, or of the Bible's tendency in Samuel to give us snapshots without regard for the narrative flow. Whatever the reason, Saul is now about to notice him.

Divested of armor, David is ready. Goliath takes him for a harmless lad, an insult to his own prowess. The reader knows better. English poet Edmund Blunden, in his memoir of World War I, called himself a "harmless young shepherd in a soldier's coat." David is quite the reverse—a skilled young soldier in the frock of a shepherd. David's skill is not unprecedented; the book of Judges tells us that an elite core of Benjaminites (Saul's tribe, in fact) "could sling a stone at a hair, and not miss" (Judg. 20:16).

Modern ballistics experts have calculated the lethal velocity of a stone hurled by an expert with a slingshot. David and Goliath trade imprecations and then David lets his stone fly. Unerringly hitting the one place on Goliath not covered by armor, the stone strikes his forehead and the giant falls forward. This apparent violation of physics—the force should have driven him back—has given interpreters some trouble. Perhaps he stumbled and fell forward. But it may also be the Tanach's way of reminding us that David's actions evoke contraries: Saul, whom he will usurp, loves him. Saul's son Jonathan, whose place David will assume, loves him. He will fraternize with the enemy and neither they nor Israel seem to turn on him as a result. His adulterous affair will produce a son who grows to be his successor. David does not operate by the normal physics of human consequence. His stone hits and the stricken fall forward.

Scholars who study ancient armor have posited that Philistine helmets in fact left a gap at the forehead. The Rabbis, also bothered by this detail (why was Goliath not better protected?) give a slightly more fanciful explanation. When David, during the trading of insults, tells Goliath that he will give his flesh to "the birds of the heaven and the beasts of the earth" (1, 17:46), Goliath looks up involuntarily at the mention of birds, and his helmet, slipping, gives David his chance. The Septuagint, the early Greek translation of the Bible (also known as LXX, for seventy) avoids the problem by saying the stone went through the helmet.

The Goliath story is a deliberate and subtle introduction to David. He plays the naïf with his brother. David's playacting will be a critical component in his personal arsenal as the story proceeds. He moves from innocence with his older brother to advertising his willingness to fight Goliath so effectively that the troops report his words to Saul. He then persuades Saul to send him as a representative of Israel, demonstrating the eloquence that will aid him many times in the future. Through it all, the young man's adeptness at combat is decisive. When he says to Saul that he has bested beasts, he is reminding us that he is a skilled killer. Finally there is an element of deception that displays clear cunning. David, it is assumed by everyone, will attack with a sword. When he does not, Goliath taunts him, "Am I a dog that you come at me with sticks?" This is presumably David's staff, and perhaps Goliath is assuming David will use his staff to attack. But David is concealing his real weapon, the slingshot. Had Goliath anticipated it, a shield would effectively have rendered it useless. David's eloquence, nerve, deception, ruthlessness (he wields Goliath's own sword to cut off the Philistine's head; the stone only knocked him out), and triumph are all elements of the king we will come to know.

The coda to the story is also telling. David brings Goliath's head to Jerusalem (though this seems an anachronism, since Jerusalem was not yet an Israelite city) and puts Goliath's weapons in his tent. In part this is foreshadowing (Goliath's sword will play a role later in the story), but it reminds us that David is already claiming the prizes of victory. This may be convention, but it is also character. More striking than if David recounted the story as a fireside yarn on a cold night, the symbol of the legendary warrior he slew is visible to any visitor. David's proverbial mantelpiece tells his story.

Heroic moments are irresistible to artists. The slaying of Goliath has drawn some of art's greatest masters: Michelangelo, Caravaggio, Rubens, Rembrandt, and countless others. In each rendering David is a shining youth, self-assured in triumph. In the twentieth century, the image of young David served in antifascist and Holocaust art to represent resistance to the more powerful foe.

Three people are described as "big" in the David story: his older brother Eliab, rejected for the kingship; Goliath, slain by David; and Saul, whose kingship will be lost to David. David is, by contrast, small but beloved, symbolic of Israel. The ability to overcome those who are apparently more formidable provides a backdrop of God's favor. Younger sons will triumph over the older and small nations over the larger, for when earthly expectations are confounded, God's hand is shown.

After David's triumph it is natural for Saul to be somewhat wary of the boy. Of course, even should Saul prove inadequate to the task of leadership, kingships are generally hereditary. What will Saul's children think of this upstart who seems poised to cause disruption in the royal house?

Immediately following the story of Goliath we read that the soul of Saul's son Jonathan became bound up with the soul of David and that Jonathan loved him as himself. No cause is given, although we are entitled to assume that David's dash and brio in vanquishing Goliath may have been sufficient. Jonathan also may have witnessed David's skill in easing his father's melancholy. David is singularly easy to love: In this single chapter (1, 18) Jonathan, the people, and Michal are all said to love David. Of course, the search for explanations of deep friendship or love is always futile, the answer ever inadequate. No constellation of virtues alone ensures that one will be loved. It could be the case for Jonathan, as the essayist Montaigne wrote in his elegy for his closest friend, Étienne de La Boétie, "If you press me to say why I loved him, I can say no more than because he was he, and I was I."

Jonathan and David's relationship has been the subject of a great deal of speculation and assertion, much of it having more to do with the writer's agenda than with the biblical story. On the one hand, both the declaration of Jonathan's attachment and the statement in David's later eulogy, "More wondrous your love to me / than the love of women," are easily construed as evidence of a sexual relationship. Additionally, Saul's angry accusation to Jonathan, "You have chosen the son of Jesse to your own shame and the shame of your mother's nakedness" (1, 20:30), has been plausibly interpreted as an accusation of sexual intimacy. However, if the taboo against homosexuality was as strong as we infer from other biblical texts, then it is hard to believe that the biblical author assumed the relationship would be understood sexually. We do know that in earlier ages men expressed themselves romantically toward other men without the implication of sexuality, in the manner of Shakespeare's York and Suffolk at Agincourt: "He threw his wounded arm, and kissed his lips, / And so espous'd to death, with blood he seal'd / a testament of noble-ending love."

Charm is a quality with sexual currents. The David who charmed so many in his journey clearly charmed Jonathan as well. Separate from a given reader's agenda, we simply cannot know whether the allusions were intended to be taken romantically; there is sufficient warrant to argue either way.

The recurring question is this—was David himself charmed? Was the love reciprocal? We read that Jonathan's soul became bound up with David, and even in his eulogy David speaks of the dearness of Jonathan's love, but confesses to no love of his own. He declares that Jonathan was "very dear" to him. Although David is described repeatedly as being loved, he is pointedly never described as loving.

The vanquishing of Goliath offers an instant etched in our memory: David is young, captivating, and full of promise. This is the David that Michelangelo chose for his famous sculpture. This is the David who seems magically to make himself beloved, not only of the king and his family and the people of Israel, but of God. Later there will be hatred and revenge and swampy motives that crisscross a life of power, lust, and war. Yet at this sunlit moment, David carrying off the sword of Goliath, we should pause to behold one of the most enchanting creations the world has to display: a young man charismatic and bold, charming and assured, astonishing in his gifts and touched by an inexplicable grace that the Bible calls the favor of God.

David's mother is not named in the text. David's father, as we have seen, forgot to introduce him to Samuel. When David found a substitute father in Saul, he found someone who would, repeatedly, seek to kill him.

Later we will see David as a father. His record in that role is, to say the least, undistinguished. But for the moment pause to consider David the child, a person of extraordinary gifts who nonetheless languishes unnoticed. Such an upbringing is a breeding ground both for resentments and for dreams. History does not lack examples of future kings dismissed by their fathers; we have a sad note from the future Frederick the Great beseeching his father to stop hating him. And the Tanach itself offers parallels in those who suffer from their families of origin only to triumph in the wider world.

Many commentators have noticed similarities between the Joseph story and the David story: the rise from humble beginnings, the child with special talents, family strife, and the drama of rulership. But although the two shared sibling tensions, Joseph was favored by his father. David was slighted.

Psalms offers some evidence (Ps. 69: "I have become a stranger to my brothers, an alien to my mother's sons"). The Psalms may not always reflect David's life, and his authorship is uncertain at best. Still, repeatedly we find that certain Psalms appear to open a pathway to David's inner life, and here they prove illuminating. The one reference we have to interaction with his brothers is right before the encounter with Goliath. His eldest brother Eliab makes condescending remarks accusing him of impudence and wickedness. So we can imagine that David not only was neglected by his parents but, like Joseph, was not beloved of his brothers. While it is true that David's anointing takes place "in the midst of his brothers" (1, 16:13), the triumph of one sibling is not notable for endearing him to the others.

So the young David, on the verge of being both celebrated and hunted, is a child who has gone from the obscurity of his home to being a sudden celebrity in Israel. He will soon learn, as so many have before him, that the hardships of neglect can pale beside the challenges of acclaim.

Shakespeare told us, "Golden lads and girls all must, as chimney sweepers, come to dust." Modern readers cannot see young David plain without knowing the travails that will beset him, the ignominious fall, the theological accruals of centuries. We cannot strip away from David who he became. Glowing, he singes others, and we remember the wounds as well as the promise. Yet one of the charms of youth is its ignorance of endings. David does not know what will happen. He is now in his ascendancy, in his unsullied glory.

What distinguishes his gifts? David throughout his life is ever capable of enlarging the image, seeing perspectives that a more blinkered view cannot imagine. When it is clear that Goliath cannot be felled with armor and sword, he envisions another possibility. Later, when Saul's pursuit makes his continued existence in Israel impossible, he flees to the enemy. When Jerusalem is a backwater, he will see it as a capital; when worship in Israel is nomadic, he will envision a Temple. David's reputation as a musician and poet reinforces this quality; he is someone who does not follow the normal paths but brings into being, conjuring solutions and possibilities from the void: In the seventeenth century, English poet Abraham Cowley wrote in his epic *Davideis*, "From the best Poet, the best of Kings did grow." When we call someone resourceful, we credit the person with drawing from what is there in useful ways. But David is beyond resourceful; he makes things new. Samuel did not see him as a king but God did, for God envisions possibilities. David is, in this sense too, a man of God.

2

Lover and Husband

A KING's loves are ever sullied by statecraft. They may be designed from the beginning to foster relations between states, a form of alliance obsessively practiced by David's son and successor Solomon, reputed to have had a thousand wives, a number more suited to bookkeeping than to romance. Even when a coupling begins with love or lust, as with David and Bathsheba, the state feels the vibrations. David's relationships with women are by far the most detailed and nuanced in the Bible. Untangling which of David's marriages were strategic and which fueled by love may be impossible. An unmixed motive does not seem to exist in David's world, or in his heart. He imperils his kingdom through raw desire but also marries with an eye toward advancement. His relations to women are at least as complex as all the other arenas of his life. This ancient king, although with royal inflections, reminds us of our own conflicted natures.

David's first recorded encounters with women are in public. After he vanquishes Goliath, women in the streets call out, "Saul has struck down his thousands/and David his tens of thousands" (1, 18:7).

This acclamation is first a threat to Saul's ascendancy. His reaction is to suspect David's intentions from that moment forward, a suspicion with tragic consequences. It is significant that jealousy begins with the cheers of women. Suddenly, a young boy, who was yesterday a shepherd, is the darling of Israel's women. We know nothing from the text of David's mother, not even her name, although the Rabbis spin tales of her love for him. Whatever David's previous experience may have been, from this moment forward women will be instrumental in shaping his story. Their adoration, advice, and comfort will appear at crucial moments throughout David's life.

Saul has not become king without learning the potential of women to make or break men in power. Saul seeks ways to eliminate David. He has been so crude as to clumsily and ineffectively launch his own spear at the nimble youth. Now the king decides on a different approach. Saul resolves to arrange a marriage not as statecraft but as sabotage. But when Saul seeks to use women to upend David, it does not work; David will parry Saul's attacks, only to prove far more successful in upending himself.

Wary of the growing popularity of the upstart, Saul resolves to give David the hand of his eldest daughter, Merab, in return for David's promise to fight against the Philistines. David ponders the offer with a becomingly modest demurral ("Who am I and who are my kin, my father's clan in Israel, that I should be the king's son-in-law?" [1, 18:18]). Is he speaking from genuine humility or from well-founded suspicion? Since we are not clear exactly what campaign Saul was requesting, David may also have been wary of undertaking a perilous mission. While he dithers, Merab is betrothed to another.

David has been told on the battlefield that Saul has promised his daughter to the man who slays Goliath. At least one biblical commentator, Abravanel, assumes that Merab chose her mate without her father's knowledge. No matter; the way is now cleared for the younger daughter Michal, for "the daughter of Saul loved David" (1, 18:20).

This is the single instance in the Hebrew Bible of a woman being said to love a man, a tribute to David's appeal. Both Jonathan and Michal, Saul's children, are said to love David. Love in its nature is transgressive, it overspills boundaries. Part of the engine of devotion could well have been the clear threat that he posed to their father, and even their father's hostility toward him. They would not be the first children to choose companions guaranteed to antagonize their parents. They may have truly loved and cared for their father as well as loving David. The story of David continually reminds us that little if anything in human relations is entirely wholehearted, and to speak of a conflicted heart is simply to speak of a human heart.

It is not clear who tells Saul of Michal's love for David; the Hebrew reads "when they" reported it. "They" could be the servants. It could be members of his household; in a scene worth imagining, Merab and Michal together may have informed their father, one disdaining David and the other claiming him. Either way, Saul is pleased, thinking Michal "would be a snare" and enable Saul to set David against the Philistines. Saul is not above using his national enemies to eliminate his personal foe. (Later, David will use just such a tactic to dispose of his lover's husband, Uriah.) Saul sends his servants to persuade David to accept the offer of marrying Michal.

An overarching question throughout the book of Samuel is David's legitimacy as king. The royal line was assumed in the ancient world as today to be hereditary, yet David will supplant the line of Saul, earlier chosen by God through Samuel. David's marriage to Michal is an opportunity to unite the two lines and establish his children the legitimate heirs to the crown.

Broadly speaking, David represented Judah in the South and Saul was the favorite of Israel in the North. Michal is in Saul's eyes a trap, in David's a golden chance. It has been justly said that every action Saul takes, benevolent or antagonistic, works in David's favor. And conversely but complementarily, everything David does, wittingly or not, paves his path to the crown. Saul is about to devise a plan to ensure that the Philistines kill David. Yet in the end David will become king when the Philistines kill Saul. When the Bible declares that God was with David, the reader, having seen each spun thread turn to gold, understands the force of the statement.

Saul springs the "trap"—all David needs for a bride price is the foreskin of a hundred Philistines. In a coup that surely ratchets up the dread in Saul's heart, David and his men strike down two hundred Philistines. Not the most idyllic wedding gift ever devised, but effective.

The condition having been dramatically fulfilled, David's relationship with Michal begins in drama and rescue. Saul, increasingly fearful of his son-in-law, is intent on eliminating him. As the Elizabethan poet Michael Drayton writes, "Melancholy/craz'd his wits." Saul resolves to put David to death, not in a haphazard burst of anger, as has happened so far—twice he tried to pin David against the wall with a spear and twice David evaded the blow—but systematically. Saul sends messengers to David's house to keep watch, so that he can execute David in the morning. Michal warns her husband: "If you do not get yourself away tonight, you will be killed in the morning" (1, 19:11). Michal then lowers David from the window and he escapes. She replaces his body in bed with a household idol and a thatch of goat's hair. The fact that she had an idol on hand not only recalls the story of Rachel hiding her father's household gods (Gen. 31) but reminds us that idolatry was slow to be expunged from Israel. This is unsurprising to those who take Israel's prophets seriously, because the prophets are constantly rebuking the people for idolatry. They would not rage against violations no one was committing. Idolatry had deep roots and was slowly unearthed from the soil of Israel's worship. When archeologists excavate ancient Israelite sites, they invariably find a cache of idols, small stone carved figures, primarily fetishes intended to help fertility. That Michal had an idol on hand is a shock to piety but a commonplace to history.

Michal's fealty to David is a nervous one, however. She may love him, but her position as a woman buffeted by kings present and future is uneasy. The dilemma of women caught between fathers and husbands is not new, but the crown intensifies the stakes of each encounter. When her father reproaches her for protecting his enemy, she lies. She reports that David threatened her life: "He said to me: 'Let me go. Why should I kill you?'" (1, 19:17). The lie reinforces Saul's negative image of David but spares Michal.

David flees and Michal languishes. Marriage to a fugitive consigns her to distance that will never entirely be bridged. In his flight through the countryside Michal's husband finds other wives. Later we discover that, in revenge, Saul has nullified David's marriage to Michal and wed her to a man named Paltiel.

While Saul seeks to end David's life, we begin to see David's natural capacity for leadership. He becomes the captain of a roaming, ragtag band. As the youngest son he can expect no inheritance, but David is more than capable of providing for himself. When they discover that Nabal, a wealthy man in the vicinity of Hebron in Judah, has shepherds grazing in the area, David and his men undertake a sort of pastoral protection racket. They watch out over the sheep and the shepherds—a project more dangerous than it sounds. Ancient Israel was a place where both man and beast were constantly threatening. Recall that in presenting himself as a candidate to fight Goliath, David boasted that he has defeated both bear and lion. Not all shepherds were adept at defense, and such safeguarding was presumably required, since all flocks faced the same perils. Skilled fighters are always needed. David asks in return for whatever Nabal can give to him and his men. David's speech uses "shalom," peace, three times. It is not combative or aggressive. His protection may be unsolicited, but for the shepherds it is surely not unwelcome. Their master Nabal feels differently.

Nabal is incensed at the idea that he should "take my bread and my water and my meat that I slaughtered for my shearers and give it to men who come from I know not where?" (1, 25:11). Nabal, without the benefit of the *Godfather* movies, does not understand offers one cannot refuse, but he is about to learn the inevitable result of spurning David. As a settled landowner he simply has failed to reckon with the daring that was second nature to his foe, or with his desperation. David's reaction is unambiguous: "Every man, gird his sword!" David goes with four hundred men (the same number Esau took to meet his brother Jacob, whom he had sworn to kill), while two hundred stayed behind with the gear. David, in the coarse rhetoric of the warrior, vows, "Thus may God do to David and even more, if I leave from all that is his until morning a single pisser against the wall!" (1, 25:23). David's band is planning a massacre.

Here the Bible offers a rare speech by an unnamed participant that clarifies the situation. One of the lads—that is, one of Nabal's shepherds—says to Abigail, whom we now meet as Nabal's wife: "Look, David sent messengers from the wilderness to greet our master, and he pounced on them. And the men [that is, David's men] have been very good to us and we were not humiliated and we missed nothing the whole time we went about with them, when we were out in the field. They were a wall around us both night and day the whole time we were with them tending the sheep. And now, mark and see what you must do, for the evil is resolved against our master and against all his house, and he is such a scoundrel no one can speak to him" (1, 25:14–17).

Nabal is despised by his own household—not only by his employees but by his wife, Abigail. The shepherds recognize a certain justice in David's demands. And Abigail now undertakes some skillful diplomacy. She begins by approaching David with bread, wine, sheep, grain, and cakes, all mounted on donkeys, in another echo of Jacob's approaching Esau with gifts.

Abigail is the first woman in Tanach to be described by her mind before her appearance: "The woman had a good mind and lovely looks" (1, 25:3). She now demonstrates the suppleness of her mind, standing before David. Abigail gives a speech, the longest prose speech by any woman in all of Scripture, in which she prostrates herself, denigrates her husband, and appeals to David's vanity, nobility, and cupidity:

> And she flung herself at his feet and said, "Mine, my lord, is the blame! But let your servant speak in your ears, and hear the words of your servant. Pray, let not my lord pay mind to this scoundrel of a man, to Nabal, for just like his name, he is, his name means Base and baseness is with him. And as for me, your servant, I never saw my lord's lads whom you sent. And now, my lord, as the Lord lives and as you live—the Lord Who kept you from coming into blood guilt with your own hand delivering you—and now, like Nabal may your enemies be who seek evil against my lord. And now, this blessing that your servant has brought to my lord, let it be given to the lads who go about in the footsteps of my lord. Forgive, pray, the crime of your servant, for the Lord will surely make for my lord a stalwart house, for he fights the battles of the Lord and no evil will be found in you for all your days. And when a person rises to pursue you, to seek your life, my lord's life will be bound in the bundle of the living with the Lord your God, and the lives of your enemies He will sling from the hollow of the sling. And so, when the Lord does for my lord all the good that He has spoken about you and He appoints you prince over Israel, this will not be a stumbling block and a trepidation of the heart to my lord, to have shed blood for

no cause and for my lord to have carried out his own deliverance, then will the Lord do well with my lord, and you will remember your servant." (I, 25:24–32).

The skill of this speech is in the continual self-abasement, in the insistent puffery ("lord" appears in the Hebrew fourteen times), its implicit promise, and its appeal to David's better side before his men, subtly reminding him that earlier he might have killed Saul but did not. Entering the kingship with soiled hands will not serve David's ultimate aims. Perhaps even the speech's length is a product of calculation, giving David time to cool. The Midrash praises Abigail's action: "Abigail [in preventing David from sinning] was better for David than all the sacrifices in the world which atone for sins after they have been committed" (Midrash Socher Tov, 53:1).

David acquiesces, and Abigail returns home to find her husband drunk. She tells Nabal nothing, but when he wakes in the morning, she recounts what occurred. Nabal then has a well-timed heart attack, and dies.

As will recur repeatedly throughout the story, an enemy of David's dies with no apparent responsibility on his part. It has not escaped careful readers of the Tanach that Abigail's concluding remark is: "You will remember your servant." Many see that as an explicit appeal, or prediction, of the time when Abigail will be available to David. Whether she or he had any hand in bringing about the result we cannot know. One can say only that the timing of Nabal's coronary is opportune in the extreme.

The moment David hears of Nabal's demise, he blesses God and sends for Abigail as his wife. She is summoned and responds instantly. Although enveloped in almost courtly drama, the marriage proves economically important to David's burgeoning ambitions. With the marriage of Abigail and the assumption of Nabal's lands in the South comes David's first major acquisition that helps to turn him from a marauder with a reputation into a man of substance and property. Nabal was a Calebite, a group of non-Israelites centered around Hebron that had joined with the tribe of Judah. Seven years after this incident David will create a capital in Jerusalem. At this period the capital is Hebron.

A reminder of how much is hidden from us is in the coda to this story, which reports that David had also taken another wife, Ahinoam (future mother of Amnon, David's firstborn son) and that in the meantime, "Saul had given Michal his daughter, David's wife, to Palti son of Laish, who was from Gallim" (1, 25:44). David now has three wives and Michal has two husbands. (The Rabbis, in an excess of chivalry, claim that the union between Michal and Paltiel was never consummated. They do not feel a corresponding need to claim that David was ever chaste with his multiple wives.)

Our next glimpse of Michal is later in the story, after Saul and Jonathan have died. David says to Abner, the former head of Saul's troops, that he will make a pact with him, but only if he brings Michal back to David. They have not seen each other for a long time. David sends messengers to Saul's remaining son, Ish-Bosheth. The text then offers these devastating lines:

> And Ish-Bosheth sent and took her from her husband, from Paltiel son of Laish. And her husband went with her, weeping as he went after her, as far as Bahurim. And Abner said to him, "Go back." And he went back. (2, 3:15–16)

In Paltiel we have a small, vivid glimpse of a man caught between historical titans. The woman he loves is taken, for David desires the spoils of his triumph. Does love exist between David and Michal? The next and final incident in their relationship suggests otherwise.

David has triumphed in battle and succeeded in bringing the ark back from its capture by the Philistines. This might be his most exalted moment as a warrior, but success does not always endear us to estranged spouses. The story is told of Samuel Beckett that he knew his marriage was over when his wife answered the phone and exclaimed, "Quelle catastrophe!" When he asked her what had happened, she informed him that he had won the Nobel Prize.

> And as the Ark of the Lord came into the City of David, Michal the daughter of Saul looked out through the window and saw King David leaping and whirling before the Lord, and she scorned him in her heart. (2, 6:16)

Note the identifiers: the ark is God's, the city is David's, Michal is Saul's. The near-Homeric tags already inform us that Michal is not, primarily, the wife of David. She who once saved him by lowering him through a window now peers through another window and sees the man who ran away, succeeded her father, stripped her of her loving husband Paltiel, cavorting in frenzied triumph. It is too much. This time, the window is not an escape, it is the porthole of a prison: "And Michal daughter of Saul came out to meet David, and she said, 'How honored today is the king of Israel who has exposed himself today to the eyes of his servants' slavegirls as some scurrilous fellow would expose himself!' And David said to Michal, 'Before the Lord, Who chose me instead of your father and instead of all his house, to appoint me prince over the Lord's people, over Israel, I will play before the Lord! And I will be dishonored still more than this and debased in my own eyes. But with the slavegirls about whom you spoke; with them let me be honored!' And Michal daughter of Saul had no child until her dying day" (2, 6:20–23).

The implication is that David no longer lay with Michal and she withered. There is a strange, ambiguous afterword to the story. Long after the death of Saul, David hands his descendants, including "the five sons of Michal, daughter of Saul," over to the Gibeonites, who kill them. The Septuagint, the early Greek rendering of the text, has "Merab" (the oldest daughter of Saul whom David was to marry but did not). Three possibilities, in ascending order of likelihood: that David handed over his own children conceived with Michal; that he handed over Michal and Paltiel's children; or, most probably, that he handed over Merab's children and the text earlier was correct that Michal never bore offspring. Yet even if the insertion here of Michal's name is a scribal error, it is also a final insult to the memory of a woman who suffered from being trapped between a powerful, vengeful father and a powerful, vengeful husband. An unhappy fate.

There is a fourth option, favored by both Josephus and rabbinic literature, that Merab died and Michal raised her sister's children, hence their designation as Michal's children. She who was born of a king and is the first woman in the Bible said to love a man, she who once saved David's life, ends up discarded and alone. In a book rife with candidates for the harshest fate, Michal's is surely as bitter as any.

The stories of Abigail and Michal are more detailed than almost any we have between men and women in the Bible. In both we see a mix of design and desire on David's part. He is in control, and the women in his life contribute in some way to his increasing stature as king. Michal ties him to Saul, and Abigail grants him property. Each is given a voice and character of her own, however; we are never to think that David's is the only will that matters.

If we were following the narrative straight, we would have reached a point where David is now undisputed king. Later on we will explore the crisis of his kingship which involves a third and most significant woman in David's life. We have learned enough with Michal and Abigail to draw some tentative conclusions about David, to be tested against the continuation of his story.

Watching his progress to the kingship, it is fair to wonder whether this young man who has suffered slights but not failure, disappointment but not inadequacy, has the emotional maturity and vulnerability to love. For more than is true for any other character in the Bible, David's psychology and Israel's history are inextricable. The personal choices he makes determine the fate of his people.

When we think of most characters, the relational life of each is bound up with one other person: Romeo and Juliet, Damon and Pythias, Naomi and Ruth. But David's life is multivalent: David and Jonathan, David and Bathsheba, David and Saul, David and Joab, David and Michal, David and Solomon —he has a range of important relationships that make up not only his story but Israel's history. And almost all of them are marked by some wreckage or despair.

They are never just ruin alone, however. There is continually in his life another road: David's path is often blocked, but only for a time, before God opens new possibilities.

What we learn reinforces many of our images of David, and reveals some disturbing new aspects of character. We know he is capable of using those around him for his own ends. He leaves Michal behind to face her father's wrath, encourages Jonathan to protect him from Saul, threatens Nabal, and ends up inheriting his property.

There is a coarse utilitarianism about the way David conducts himself. And yet throughout his dealings there also run currents of deep emotion.

David's marriage to Michal begins in some combination of love and calculation and ends embittered. Abigail escapes to David from a cruel husband. To neither will David express love. None of his wives is remembered in his final words. Yet to each he will listen and react; all of them will break through the isolation of the king's state in a way we do not read about with Saul or with Solomon. David may not have let women fully into his heart, but neither did he keep them at arm's length. A poet, a musician, a multiply married man, he understood the tropes and obligations of attachment, and with his wives as with his children, as we shall see, closeness to others determined his destiny even as it divided his heart.

3

Fugitive

ABRAHAM MENDELSSOHN was the son of famed philosopher Moses Mendelssohn and the father of composer Felix
Mendelssohn. Though a banker of some note himself, in his
later years he lamented that the first half of his life he was the
son of his father, and the second half of his life, the father of his
son. The story of David is an inversion of Mendelssohn. David
is the eminence between two failures: His tale is divided between two extended episodes, the kingship that he took from
Saul, his substitute father (he even calls Saul "my father" [1,
24:12]), and the rebellion he fended off from Absalom, his son.

After David's conquest of Goliath the huzzahs echoed in
Israel, praising David's accomplishments. Their portent is
plain: "And Saul kept a suspicious eye on David from that day
hence" (1, 18:9). Remembering the bouts of melancholy which
brought Saul to summon David as an unknown musician suggests the possibilities of darkness that exist when Saul feels

threatened by a young man whom he has welcomed into his own home.

As David is playing in his house, Saul takes a spear and seeks to impale David. "And David eluded him twice" (I, 18:11). In a sly allusion to Saul's ineffectiveness, the same verb (hikah) used by the women to declare at the outset of David's service in Saul's army that "Saul struck down his thousands / and David his tens of thousands," is used now for Saul's misfired strike against David. There exists a linguistic as well as a narrative connection between David's popular acclaim and Saul's jealous rage.

What can it mean that David twice eluded him? Would one attempt not persuade him to flee? Did he think Saul could be calmed after the first outburst, only to discover that his rage recurred? Or perhaps, in an image that is most suggestive of the gap between them, did David find it easy to elude Saul and therefore feel no need to run?

The text continues, "And David succeeded in all his ways, and the Lord was with him. And Saul saw that he was very successful, and he dreaded him. But all Israel and Judah loved David, for he led them into the fray" (I, 18:15–16).

David is now almost universally loved, the irresistible man. "Love" in ancient Hebrew has accents of loyalty. Soldiers do on occasion love their generals, but more important is that the one who leads them into battle can command loyalty. Saul's spirit may have been dark and paranoid, but his understanding was keen: Anyone who has the loyalty of his troops poses a threat to his leadership.

Remember that Saul now proposes that David marry his eldest daughter, Merab, but David marries Michal, Saul's second daughter, after slaying two hundred Philistines as a bride price. Saul, witnessing David meet this outlandish demand, is still more terrified of the prodigal soldier.

Yet David is protected by influential advocates. Following

David's flight—once it is clear that Saul wants his head—Jonathan, Saul's son, David's confidant and friend, approaches his father. He pleads David's case, saying that David has been good for Saul, good for Israel. When his son finishes speaking, Saul swears, "As the Lord lives, he shall not be put to death." Jonathan brings David back to Saul, "And he served him as in times gone by" (1, 19:7).

But jealousy is not an easily cured affliction, and Saul is still unstable. In short order he seeks once again to kill David. Michal helps her husband to slip away. David will no longer trust the perilous confines of Saul's house. Now he is a fugitive on the run from the king of Israel. What David does to survive, controversial and at times unclear, will help shape his legacy.

His own immediate family is no safe refuge. David runs instead to Samuel, the priest and prophet who anointed him long ago when he came to the house of David's father, Jesse. When Saul hears that David is staying with Samuel in the city of Naioth, he goes off in pursuit. As happens so often in the story of David, it is hard to see how he might escape.

On his mission to find and kill David, Saul sends prospective assassins to find him in Naioth. Apparently, prophecy can prove contagious: Each man whom Saul sends becomes himself enmeshed in the prophetic vocation that is the business of the city, offering prophecies instead of eliminating rivals. Finally, Saul himself heads to Naioth. He, too, is visited by a bout of prophetic ecstasy. Saul strips off his clothes and lies naked before Samuel. While nakedness is not unknown among the prophets—Isaiah walks naked and barefoot for three years (Is. 20:3)—the picture both reinforces Saul's instability and symbolizes the way he is being stripped of his kingdom. Saul's sudden prophecy, sapping his effectiveness as a pursuer, reminds us once again that God's hidden hand protects his newly anointed. While Saul is enraptured, David slips away.

Fearful for his life, David again enlists Saul's son Jonathan to help him. Jonathan must have secret channels of communication to know where David is while his father seeks him. Much of the book will play on just this sharing of information, on secrecy and spying. In a civilization where the overwhelming burden of communication was on oral messages from one to another, trust was essential. Messengers could betray, or be coerced into revealing secrets. Kings and fugitives must know upon whom they can depend. The trialogue between Jonathan, David, and Saul, chapter 20 in the book of Samuel, is a roundelay in which Jonathan discovers that his father will not spare David and chooses to offer his loyalty to the hunted.

Jonathan and David resolve upon a sign. If Saul continues to threaten David at his home, Jonathan will secretly alert David by the way he instructs his servants to fetch the arrows he will shoot for sport near David's hiding place.

The first day that David was missing from his usual spot at Saul's table, Saul had dismissed it as indisposition, that is, ritual uncleanliness. But the second time, when Jonathan made an excuse for him, he bore the wrath of his father: "O, son of a perverse wayward woman! Don't I know you have chosen the son of Jesse to your own shame and the shame of your mother's nakedness? For as long as the son of Jesse lives on the earth you and your kingship will not be unshaken. And now, send and fetch him to me, for he is a dead man" (1, 20:30–31).

When Jonathan pleads David's case, "What has he done?" Saul throws a spear at his own son. Now Jonathan grasps the irrationality of his father's hatred. "And Jonathan rose from the table in burning anger, and he ate no food on the second day of the new moon because he was pained for David and because his father had humiliated him" (1, 20:34).

Each action that Saul takes against David redounds to David's benefit. Saul is losing his family, his kingship, and increasingly, his sanity.

Jonathan goes out into the field and sends the signal. Jonathan affirms what David already knows: He can never go back. "Each man kissed the other and each wept for the other, though David the longer. And Jonathan said to David, 'Go in peace, for the two of us have sworn in the name of the Lord, saying, "The Lord is witness between me and you, and between my seed and your seed, for all time"'" (1, 20:41–42).

Jonathan is a fair candidate for noblest character in the David story. As the seventeenth-century English poet Abraham Cowley beautifully writes:

> He is such a freind (such Acts can freindship doe)
> The Crowne did yeild, and kept the freindship too.
> Which cleerely prov'd he for a Crowne was fit,
> If but because soe well he yeilded it.

Jonathan might indeed have made a worthy king, as Cowley writes, since kings are so rarely endowed with the penchant for self-sacrifice. But in addition to whatever personal fidelity existed between them, Jonathan saw in David qualities he did not possess and wanted to save his friend.

Word doubtless spread quickly in ancient Israel, though a fugitive could stay a few steps ahead of the rumors. David's first stop on his long flight is at Nob, south of Gibeah, where the "trembling" priest Ahimelech asks why he travels alone. In response to the nervous inquiry, David lies, claiming that he is on a confidential mission from the king. When he asks for food, Abiathar answers that there is only the consecrated bread—loaves set out for later consumption by the priests—but gives them to a hungry David.

Now David asks for a spear or sword: "For neither my sword nor my gear have I taken with me for the king's mission was urgent" (1, 21:19). It happens that Goliath's sword, which we last saw in David's tent, has found its way here. When Ahimelech offers it, David answers, "There is none like it. Give it to me." So David, who could not wear the armor or bear the arms of

Saul, who was tall but no giant, is now capable of wielding Goliath's sword, the ancient analogue of Babe Ruth's bat. As we imagine him unsheathing it, there is a clear Excalibur theme: The one who can wield this sword is a full warrior and to be feared.

The territory of Israel is not safe. David flees west, to Philistine territory, Goliath's sword in hand. When he is presented before the Philistine king Achish, the Philistine fighters recognize him as a renowned warrior in Israel. Facing this new threat, David, ever resourceful, begins to feign madness: "And he altered his good sense in their eyes and played the lunatic before them, and he scrabbled on the doors of the gate and drooled onto his beard. And Achish said, 'Look, do you see this man is raving mad! Why would you bring him to me?'" (1, 21:15).

The Rabbis spin a parable from this, telling stories of how David, suffering from Saul's crazed pursuit, asked God how God could create madness in the world. Now his life is saved by the existence of madness. Psalm 34 contains the superscription "A Psalm of David when he feigned madness . . . " The Rabbis note that the psalm begins, "I bless the Lord at all times." In other words, David is blessing God even for times of madness or exile. The psalm illustrates that in this life-threatening crisis David finds the reality of God's presence. "The Lord is close to the brokenhearted, and those whose spirit is crushed God delivers" (Ps. 34:19).

Deliverance by the madness David once derided is parallel to the first story of David I remember as a child, the tale the Rabbis tell of David wondering why God would make spiders. Later, as David sleeps in a cave, hiding from Saul, a spider weaves a web over the mouth of the cave. When Saul passes the cave, he decides not to look in—for the web is undisturbed, suggesting that no one can be there. David awakes and praises all of God's creations. The midrashic message of the spider aligns with David's earlier escape by madness: Everything works in David's favor because God has chosen him to succeed. David may tax the divine largesse, but he will never exhaust it.

For the modern reader, this story of a young man who claims the throne, who comes upon an enemy who is unaware of his presence yet forgoes revenge, and who feigns madness may sound familiar, right down to the villainous substitute father figure. Did the tropes of David's story influence *Hamlet*? How much Shakespeare borrowed from the biblical David is impossible to say. (*Henry V* bears striking thematic resemblances as well.) Even Hamlet's legendary indecisiveness might derive from David, who in his dilatory response to family will seed catastrophe. Every April, Elizabethans read the book of Samuel in church, so each year around his birthday the young Shakespeare would hear of David's coronation. Repeatedly David's story casts glints of light on later figures in literature.

Now in Philistine territory, the fugitive still traverses a perilous world. No longer in the cocoon of family or royalty, he must fend for himself. Rather than being protected by his family, he now assumes responsibility for their safety, asking the king of Moab to shelter David's father and mother. The king acquiesces, perhaps because Saul had defeated Moab in an earlier war, so the Moabites have an affinity for Saul's enemies. But also we should recall that according to the book of Ruth (4:17–22) David is the great-grandson of Moabites. So he has roots, and his parents still closer roots, in Moab. His need to safeguard their welfare carries an ugly implicit message, that his family would not be safe from Saul were they within reach.

Doeg, Saul's herdsman who has witnessed the priests of Nob helping David when he was hungry, reports to Saul. Saul goes immediately to Nob and condemns the priests to death. Ahimelech protests, justly, that he had believed David to be on a mission for Saul and had assumed that Saul and David were close. Saul closes his ears to reason and commands his men to put the priests to the sword. Saul's own men shrink from the noxious command, so the spy Doeg personally slaughters eighty-five priests on the king's behalf: "And he struck down Nob the priests' town with the edge of the sword, man and woman, infant and suckling, ox and donkey and sheep, all by the edge of the sword" (1, 22:19). In this collusion between the paranoid and the sadist, almost one hundred innocents are massacred. One man gets away, Abiathar, the son of Ahimelech, the priest who had helped David. He escapes to tell David the news.

David is crushed by his part in the calamity. Here we see the unvarnished emotional anguish and empathy of the man who at other moments seems impervious to pain. David responds that as soon as he saw Doeg that day, he knew Doeg would report to Saul. "I am the one who caused the loss of all the lives of your father's house. Do not fear, for whoever seeks my life seeks your life, so you are under my guard" (1, 22:22–23).

Evasion teaches David the precariousness of life as a wanted man. Despite his success in defeating the Philistines who threaten the town of Keilah, David is not safe there. When he asks God whether the nobles of the town will hand him over to Saul, he receives an unambiguous divine response: "They will hand you over" (1, 23:11).

A range of cities are encompassed in David's wanderings. They are of interest to the scholar and cartographer, but the names themselves are less gripping for the general reader than the dramas and implications of each stop. In Ziph, near Saul's home of Gibeah, David meets up with Jonathan one more time. There is no question any longer of Saul's being other than murderously jealous of David. Jonathan speaks reassuringly to his friend: "Do not fear, for the hand of Saul my father shall not find you, and it is you who shall reign over Israel, and I on my part will be your viceroy, and even Saul my father knows it" (1, 23:17). No response from David is recorded. His silence could be one of assent, of trepidation, or of gratitude. Perhaps all these and more, since silence is large enough to contain every emotion.

Jonathan has imperfect powers of prophecy, however. While he is correct that David will escape Saul's clutches, albeit narrowly, Jonathan will not live to be David's viceroy.

In Ziph, after his encounter with Jonathan, Saul is closing in on David when he is suddenly informed of a significant Philistine invasion. He is forced to suspend his personal vendetta and fight. Once again a nearly miraculous rescue signals to the pious reader the salvific hand of God.

After Saul has fought the Philistines (we are given no details of the battle), he is told that David is hiding in the wilderness of En-gedi. En-gedi is a place of springs and caves, where a fleeing fighter could easily be concealed.

Saul steps into a cave to relieve himself, and it happens to be a cave where David and his men are hiding. David's men quietly rejoice—serendipity has struck and they can dispatch David's tormentor. Instead, David creeps up behind him and silently slices off a bit of Saul's coat. Remorseful, he tells his men that he regrets lifting even so benign a hand to God's anointed and forbids them to touch him. When Saul leaves the cave, David stands outside and calls to him. Saul looks behind and David kneels.

As he speaks, David holds up the fragment of Saul's coat. He declares that he might have killed Saul but would not lift his hand against him: "And my father, see, yes, see the skirt of your cloak in my hand." David reminds Saul of the paternal role he has played in David's life, and his unfairness: "Let the Lord judge between me and you, and the Lord will avenge me of you, but my hand will not be against you. . . . After whom are you chasing? After a dead dog, after a single flea?" (1, 24:15).

David's rhetoric is filled with both humility and the certainty of destiny. David disparages himself in colorful language. (Recall that Goliath had challenged him, "Am I a dog that you should come at me with sticks?" But at least Goliath was a live dog—David in his own words is a dead one, or a flea on a dead dog.) After belittling his own importance, he expresses his sense of destiny, telling Saul that God will exact vengeance on David's behalf. Here is the repeating and complicated calculus for any biographer of David to measure: He is rarely directly guilty in the downfall of his foes, but they do indeed fall. And the swift certainty of their fall inevitably gives rise to theories. To the faithful, it is the hand of God. To the suspicious, David's plotting. To the generous (or the credulous?), astounding luck.

Saul's response to David is charged with pathos: "'Is that your voice, my son, David?' And Saul raised his voice, and wept. And he said to David, 'You are more right than I. . . . The Lord will repay you with good for what you have done for me this day. And so, look, I know that you will surely be king and that the kingship of Israel will stay in your hands. And now, swear to me by the Lord, that you shall not cut off my seed after me and that you shall not blot out my name from my father's house.' And David swore to Saul, and Saul went home while David and his men went up to the stronghold" (1, 24:17–23).

Saul's request that David not blot out his name has both a metaphysical and a practical cast. The ancient world was witness to monuments overwritten, annals expunged, and chronicles altered in attempts to erase the names of predecessors from history. It appears in the ancient world that the only ruler who cannot be expunged is one's successor. No doubt Saul, the first king of Israel, feared being forgotten. Alongside his personal concerns was the very practical worry that his replacement would massacre his family. The resistance to David's kingship from Saul's descendants persists throughout David's life. And his fulfillment of the promise to Saul can be at best characterized as partial.

The story of David coming upon an unaware Saul recurs two chapters later. In the wilderness of Ziph, David, knowing that Saul is encamped, takes two stalwarts with him and finds Saul sleeping in his camp. Saul's military head Abner and his troops are sleeping as well. This may suggest a sort of general dereliction—surely someone should be on watch—or a misapprehension that there is no danger. They are not at battle, they are hunting a fugitive, and do not expect the fugitive to hunt them.

Abishai, brother of Joab and one of David's men, prepares to kill Saul but David restrains him. "The Lord forbid that I should reach out my hand against the Lord's anointed." Rather, David takes Saul's spear and water jug and heads off. Then from a distance he calls out to Abner and begins to taunt him:

> Are you not a man, and who is like you in Israel, and why have you not guarded your lord the king? . . . And now see, where are the king's spear and the water jug that were at his head? (1, 26:15)

Saul rises and once again is abject in his apology to David. In a strange parallel, it is as if Saul is periodically seized by demons and David still has the music to soothe him. Yet the demon that now controls him is not a generalized darkness but fear of David. Having been momentarily assuaged, both kings, the fading older king and the rising younger one, return home.

"Doublets"—paired versions of the same story—are well known in the Bible. There are two stories of Abraham passing his wife off as his sister, two creation stories, two versions of the Ten Commandments. Here the repetition of Saul's being surprised by David, who spares his life, serves both to contrast Saul and David—one murderous the other merciful—and also to prepare us for the later accusations that David secretly dispatches his enemies. Twice, the text implicitly signals, he could have slain his persecutor but did not, so why would you think this man would secretly eliminate enemies and then deny it?

In other words, since David has refrained from killing Saul, should any suspicion attach to Saul's later death in battle (and it did), David's history is a ready exoneration. Even the prompting of his troops could not move him to kill his tormentor. Rather, his tactic has been to remind Saul of the unreasonable nature of his fury. His spirit in this is captured in the Psalms: "All my enemies will be frustrated and afraid, and they shall turn back, abashed" (Ps. 6:11).

Sparing Saul is an act with more than one possible motivation. David may well have felt both a general and particular reverence to Saul. Not only was Saul the king of Israel—regicide is always a crime easier to contemplate than carry out—but Saul had taken David into his own home. The coupling of taboos, both regicide and a sort of parricide, may have been enough to stay David's hand. His warriors had no such reservations, but David did. David's recent meeting with Jonathan may also have played a role; how could he face his friend if he took his father's life? Moreover, David twice refers to Saul as God's anointed. The taboo against killing someone God has chosen is not lightly breached.

The consideration of the proper treatment of God's chosen leads to a related calculation. David is confident that Saul's reign is ending and that he himself is ascendant. It is a bad precedent to enter the kingship having killed your predecessor. People get ideas about being your successor. Once assassination is introduced into the body politic, immunization is very hard to come by. Better for David to trust in time, in God, and in Saul's increasingly frayed psyche. Supplanting Saul will be sufficiently fraught; he should enter the kingship as cleanly as possible.

Not killing Saul hardly implies trusting him. David cannot count on Saul's expressions of grief and regret. Saul will hunt him again; emotional instability has been the king's trademark characteristic since the earliest moments David played a lyre to coax him into a different state of mind. And when Saul is feeling murderous, his tenderness toward David is completely forgotten. Saul exemplifies and exaggerates the wisdom of Emerson's remark, "Our moods do not believe in each other."

So David must continue to flee. One might think he would go to Moab, where he has moved his parents. Perhaps that is too remote for David to keep his hand in the action. Whatever the motivation, the episodes that follow show clearly how complicated and uncertain is the untangling of David's story.

Among the Philistines

David flees to Israel's enemies. Once before David has come to Achish in Gath. At that time David feigned madness to escape death. Things have changed. Now his persecution by Saul has become so widely known that Achish sees in him a useful vassal. David is no longer a lone, deranged fugitive. He is a burgeoning force, together with his six hundred men and his wives, Abigail and Ahinoam. He approaches Achish and asks for a town in which to dwell. The promise is implicit: I will pay for protection. David, who earlier protected the sheep of Nabal in expectation of payment, knows the game.

Achish doles out territory like a monarch. "And Achish gave him Ziklag on that day. Therefore has Ziklag belonged to the kings of Judah until this day. And the span of time that David dwelled in Philistine country was a year and four months" (1, 27:6).

Who wrote these words? When the text tells us that Ziklag belonged to kings of Judah "until this day" it implies that it was written long after David but while there were still kings of Judah, as there were hundreds of years later. We are about to read that David conducts raids on neighboring towns. Surely the entire passage was penned, as was most of the book of Samuel, by someone who wished to vindicate David's actions. So we hear that David conducted raids on other towns from a base that did in fact belong to him, since Achish gave him the town as his own. Nonetheless, raiding from inside enemy territory is not ideal for a future king. David's raids are both the product of and the spur to opposition to his reign and the accusations that hounded him later.

David and his men "raided the Geshurite and the Gerizite and the Amalekite." In other words, he raids and loots non-Philistine tribes residing in Philistine territory. Yet he claims to Achish that he has been raiding Judah, that is, his own people. Through this subterfuge he convinces Achish that he has switched loyalties, become a traitor. In order to hide the lie, "David struck the land, and he left not a man or woman alive, and he took sheep and cattle and donkeys and camels and clothes, and he returned and came to Achish" (1, 27:9).

David wipes out entire towns and brings the booty (or a portion of it, we may presume, apart from what he kept for himself and his troops) to Achish, who is sheltering him from Saul and his own people. David destroys towns to sustain and protect himself. Abravanel argues that David's raids were a service to the Philistines as well, since those tribes troubled the Philistine people. This seems a charitable take on David's pillage. Or perhaps not so charitable, since helping the Philistines was still aiding enemies of Israel.

An author with David's best interests in mind would never tell us of David's sojourn and his massacres. This is such a distasteful tale in almost all its aspects that we must imagine it was so well known that the author did not think he could omit it. The storyteller's principal concern is to show that at no time did David in fact raid in Judah or betray his own people. This precise accusation will follow him later on. It is impossible for a king to have taken refuge and been protected for over a year in the precincts of the enemy without arousing lasting suspicion of dual loyalties. To this day some scholars have argued that David was now and later beholden to the Philistines. Surely many of David's contemporaries, chief among them the family of Saul, accuse David of being a traitor. His very ability to temporize and survive also makes the reader uneasy. As the text presents the

predicament, David has little choice. Without pretending obei-
sance and bringing booty to Achish, without acting as though he
was a turncoat, he cannot survive. In the conventional reading
it is Saul who forces David into this farce, while David remains
loyal to his people. Nonetheless, the savage raids in which he
wipes out towns in order to mislead others about his own true
loyalties remind us that the history of this precursor to the Messiah is at best one of confounding contradictions.

How can David manage to be in Achish's service, when Israel and the Philistines are mortal enemies, without eventually
fighting against his own tribe? We are told explicitly, "And Achish trusted David, saying, 'He has become repugnant to Israel
and he will be my perpetual vassal'" (1, 27:2). Not long after Achish
decides that David is his, the Philistines do indeed mobilize, and
Achish tells David that he must join the Philistine army. They are
to go to battle against Saul and the people of Israel. Will David
join them? David answers the king of the Philistines, "Then you
know what your servant will do" (1, 28:2). On this cliffhanger we
must leave David for a moment to describe one of the most per-
plexing and fascinating scenes in the Bible.

Saul Entangled in En-Dor

Several times in the book of Samuel, David asks questions
of God and is answered. God provides David with advice for
battle and speaks to him through prophets like Nathan and
Gad. As is true with a number of the most prominent biblical
figures like Moses, at times David's connection to God seems
more stable and sure than his relationship to other human beings. God and David do not exactly share a dialogue in the manner of earlier biblical characters; but although the Psalms frequently express a sense of divine abandonment, in the book of
Samuel we are told repeatedly that God is with David.

Saul, on the other hand, has enforced orthodoxy, insisting

on the worship of the one true God by proscribing the consulting of ghosts and spirits, only to discover that before a major battle with the Philistines, God will not speak to him. As was French philosopher Pascal many centuries later, Saul is terrified by the infinite spaces. The loneliness of leadership when he has been abandoned by God is too much to bear. In wild desperation Saul asks his servants to seek him out a "ghostwife," one who can conjure the dead. (She is popularly known as the necromancer or Witch of En-Dor, but "ghostwife" is a more literal translation of the Hebrew.)

The Tanach is opaque about the afterlife. The principal term, Sheol, seems to be some sort of semisleep, a shadowy existence. How one travels to Sheol is the focus—does one go there in peace or in sorrow?—rather than the destination itself. ("I will go with gray hairs in sorrow to Sheol," says Jacob, Genesis 42:38.) We have but one scene in the Bible where a character is actually summoned from the netherworld. It occurs now, on the eve of Saul's death.

The scene itself (1, 28) is full of the intrigue of Macbeth by way of Stephen King. Saul, in disguise, travels with two men at night to visit a woman and ask her to summon a ghost. She immediately suspects entrapment. Why, knowing that King Saul has forbidden necromancy, would this stranger ask her to bring forth the dead?

Saul swears by God that no harm will come to her. The woman is mollified and asks whom she should summon. Saul answers that she should raise Samuel. When she succeeds and sees Samuel before her, the ghostwife screams in a loud voice, suddenly realizing that the petitioner is Saul in disguise. Perhaps she does not believe that Samuel would disturb his repose for any less august a person. Perhaps the conjuring required a light that allowed her better to view the king. Perhaps, as some commentators both medieval and modern have it, the entire conjuration was an act.

There appears "an old man in a cloak," and Saul bows to the ground before the image of Samuel. Samuel asks, "Why have you troubled me to summon me up?" using, as Robert Alter notes, a verb that refers to sleep. Saul's answer lays bare the full measure of his distress: "I am in dire straits, and the Philistines are fighting against me and God has turned away from me and no longer answers me, neither through prophets or dreams, and I called to you to let me know what I should do" (1, 28:15).

Samuel's harsh answer to Saul confirms that God has turned away from the king and that he will fall against the Philistines: "And tomorrow—you and your sons are with me." The Israelites will lose the battle and Saul and his children will die.

The authority of Samuel's voice and the direness of the forecast overwhelm the psychologically precarious king. He collapses, both from the fast he has observed that day and from the shock of the prophecy. The ghostwife takes pity on him and encourages him to eat. (This is apparently the ancient Jewish curative for eminences in distress. When Elijah runs away to the wilderness, an angel appears and seeing his distress first says, "Eat something" [1 Kings 19:5]. And later, after the death of his first son, David ends his fast.) Israeli scholar Moshe Halbertal once remarked that he considered the Witch of En-Dor the most altruistic character in the entire chronicle and her act of nourishing the condemned king a highpoint of kindness. After initial reluctance, Saul eats with his servants, and they arise and head off into the night.

The bizarre story of Samuel's reappearance is jarring after what has been thus far a relatable, human story of power politics, family, sex, shame, and war. Samuel's summoning rekindles our appreciation for the strangeness of the world of the Bible. While it does limn—in unforgettable strokes—Saul's increasing descent into despair, violating the king's own publicly announced strictures against consulting a spirit-conjurer, it more powerfully portrays the shadows engulfing his own mind.

Jewish authorities traditionally took this scene literally, but not all the Rabbis agreed: The earliest commentator to argue that it was a deception is Samuel Ben Hofni Gaon (d. 1034). Others followed suit, arguing that the ghostwife imitated Samuel's voice and predicted Saul's demise based on what everyone knew, that he and his sons were going into a losing war with a dispirited leader. What none of the commentators doubted was that the human events were reflective of a divine plan—Saul had to die so that David could become king.

This scene has also been read as a further attempt by David's partisans to discredit Saul. Here is a broken king—violating the law of God to seek magic, rebuked even in death by Samuel, the greatest religious authority of the age—who despite his royal status has to be urged by a woman conjurer to gather the strength to eat. Such a scene makes it enormously difficult for partisans of Saul to say he was, indeed, every inch a king. Dishonor attaches to defeat, but contempt is the price of humiliation.

Leaving Saul on the eve of a fatal battle, we return to the dilemma of David. He is about to be pressed into service by Achish to fight against the Israelites; refusal will expose him as a fraud and acquiescence as a quisling. How will David manage to avoid taking sides? Salvation comes in the form of Philistine distrust.

Achish brings David before the Philistine troops, and they are enraged. They repeat back to Achish the chant of the Israelite women: "Is this not David for whom they sing out in the dances, saying 'Saul has struck down his thousands/David his tens of thousands'?" (1, 29:5).

Achish knows better than to oppose his own troops when he is preparing for combat. So he backs down and reports to David that he will have to forgo the battle due to the objections of the Philistine captains. David, continuing to play the role of eager ally, protests that he has done nothing to earn the suspicions of the Philistine troops. Achish agrees, but explains that the matter is effectively out of his hands.

Would David have fought alongside the Philistines? Classical Jewish commentators remain mostly silent on the question, with some, such as Ralbag (Rabbi Levi ben Gershon, fourteenth century), known as Gersonides, insisting that he had no intention of aiding the Philistines. Such disparate commentators as Abravanel in fifteenth-century Spain and Mezudat David in eighteenth-century Galicia do not like to think of David as betraying Achish, who had, after all, afforded him shelter. These authorities both argue that David would have provided personal protection for Achish, benefiting him individually without hurting Israel. Writing in ancient Rome, the historian and former general Josephus, who like Abravanel was in service to a hostile regime (Josephus for the Romans, and Abravanel in the government of Spanish monarchs Ferdinand and Isabella before choosing expulsion over conversion), agreed that David would have provided protection. Each believed that David would have chosen a path somewhat similar to his own. The more cynical view of modern scholars—that David was a secret mercenary for the Philistines—is probably a product of the mistrust of government characteristic of the modern age. David's choice is interpreted through the lens of each reader's experience of politics.

Yet as biblical scholar Yael Shemesh points out, it is hard to believe that David would have fought for the Philistines. Not only is his answer artfully ambiguous ("You know what your servant will do"), but he has served Saul in war for such a long time that even Jonathan attests to his loyalty to his father ("He has not wronged you" [1, 19:4]). Moreover, he has shrunk from past opportunities to harm Saul. By contrast, when it comes to the Philistine enemy, David has already fought valiantly against them (not only slaying Goliath but gathering the foreskins as Michal's bride price). Surely if David's intent was to be king, there could be no more devastating charge against him in Israel than his fighting on behalf of the Philistines. The commanders' very dismissal of David as an ally suggests that he was no friend of the Philistines, even if Achish as king had been taken in by David's wiles. Achish has already been deceived by David with regard to the raids, when he pretended to be looting Israelite towns but in fact confined his roundup to cities within the Philistine ambit. We cannot know what strategy David would have devised had he been conscripted into battle, but his invention rarely flags; the reader who has followed him thus far might feel confident that he would—with or without God's help —have managed somehow.

While David successfully evades the Philistine war, however, catastrophe strikes his home. The Amalekites, brigands and long-standing enemies of Israel, go to his temporary base in Ziklag, burn it to the ground, and take the inhabitants captive. David's wives, Ahinoam and Abigail, are among those seized, and when he and his troops return and see that their families have been taken, David's own men turn on him with murderous intent.

This is a pivotal moment in David's story. His family is abducted, his troops are furious, and he is still deep in Philistine territory. Such crises presage collapse or greatness. He is at the precipice.

The contrast of David and Saul at this moment is exquisite. When Saul was in dire straits, he had nowhere to turn. Resorting to the netherworld was an indication that this world had left him bereft of resources. But when David is assailed and effectively abandoned by his own troops, he has a more reliable otherworldly alternative to despair—God. He asks Abiathar, the priest who was saved from Saul's massacre at Nob, to bring the ephod.

The ephod was a simple garment used in conjunction with the urim and thummim, binary divining lots. While it remains unclear precisely what these forecasting materials were (they are often associated with the high priest's breastplate), we understand that one may ask yes or no questions of them. David does not really have a direct dialogue with God in the manner of earlier biblical figures such as Abraham or Moses. His is a moderated relationship, through a priest or a sign or a dream, but nonetheless sufficient both for his own purposes and to impress his followers that God is with him. Presumably, the lots must be interpreted by the priest, so if Saul felt "unanswered" earlier, it may have been that the priest sensed no response from God.

David faces a great crisis. We can only imagine the collection of loyalists, bandits, ruffians, and perhaps ecstatics who have collected around this charismatic man. He had no doubt promised, implicitly or explicitly, that when he became king their futures would be bright. Doubtless they also expected the alliance with Achish to be productive. Now everything is imperiled, their families captive, their possessions stolen. One wonders whether they feel fortunate that the treatment David had meted out to villages—killing all the men and women so that Achish might not know they were non-Israelite—is not imitated by the traditionally anathematized Amalekites, who in this case at least prefer to enslave their victims.

David asks God whether he should pursue the Amalekite raiders; he interprets the answer he receives as not only encouragement of pursuit but a guarantee of success.

David sets out with his men. He travels, as before, with four hundred soldiers, while two hundred who plead exhaustion remain behind.

The troops happen upon an Egyptian man in the field and take him to David. David feeds him and asks his story. He tells David that he was an abandoned slave who had been traveling with the Amalekites as they raided and pillaged and burned. After asking David to promise that he will be neither killed nor handed back to his master, the man agrees to tell David where the Amalekites have gone. David comes upon them sprawled out, eating and drinking, and thoroughly unprepared for an assault. David and his men, in a two-day campaign, slaughter all but four hundred "lads" who escape; the attackers recover everything and everyone, including David's two wives.

Returning home, the victorious fighters come upon the two hundred men who had been too tired to join the campaign. The soldiers begrudge their comrades any of the spoils, but the Bible judges them harshly for their greed: "And every wicked and worthless man of the men who had gone with David spoke up and said, 'Inasmuch as they did not go with us, we will give them nothing from the booty that we rescued, only each man his wife and his children, that they may drive them off and go'" (1, 30:22). Wicked and worthless they may be, but their attitude of anger toward men whose wives and children they rescued is surely understandable. David's reaction is noble, insisting that all share equally: "You must not do so, my brothers, with what the Lord has given us" (1, 30:23). David apportions the booty among his men who fought and those who, in David's own formulation, stayed with the gear. He also distributes spoils to various leaders of Judah in the cities where he traveled in and around Hebron.

A fateful war with the Philistines is coming, and now, after all that has happened, we find ourselves on the eve of Saul's death. In anticipation we have just witnessed what amounts to a full dress rehearsal for David as king. First he is miraculously spared from fighting alongside the Philistines, yet somehow—as the consummate diplomat—retains the affection of the Philistine king. Then he is faced with Amalek, an enemy who devastates his land, captures his family, and threatens the loyalty of his men. He confronts the crisis with several crucial attributes, all of which are dramatically enacted: First, he is clearly beloved of God, who answers David's agonized question about whether to pursue the enemy. Then he fortuitously finds a man, a cast-off slave, to direct him, which is either a stroke of astounding luck or a further demonstration of God's protective intervention. He directs a battle with complete success, recovering everything that had been lost and more. In his treatment of the two hundred who stay behind he demonstrates the magnanimity of a true king. Finally, in his distribution of goods to elders who had helped him, David reminds us of his political acumen.

The concluding chapter of the first book of Samuel tells of the battle against the Philistines, in which Saul will finally fall. No longer a promising youth, David is by now a battle-tempered veteran, with a group of loyalists who have fought—and remained—by his side. He has survived in hostile territory and not forgotten his base in Judah. When Saul dies, David is ready to be king.

Saul and David—God's Choice

God directs the choice of Saul as king and then regrets the decision. If we juxtapose the characters of Saul and David, we can better understand one's fall and the other's rise.

Saul's kingship is marked by misdeeds—some less grievous, such as sacrificing animals to God before Samuel arrives to superintend the ritual; some more serious, such as neglecting to kill Agag, king of the Amalekites; and some truly heinous, such as the massacre of the priests at Nob. Through it all, however, is the thread of Saul's fear.

We are told more than once that Saul fears David. "And Saul was afraid of David" (1, 18:12). And a few verses later, "And Saul was all the more afraid of David" (1, 18:29). Fear is a character trait of Saul's that reemerges in other situations as well. "And Saul saw the Philistine camp, and he was afraid, and his heart trembled greatly" (1, 28:4–6). This echoes the early story of David and Goliath. When David is brought before Saul, we are not told explicitly that he is afraid, but David's first recorded words to Saul suggest that the king might be jittery: "Let no man's heart fail him" (1, 17:32). Saul's dread of the Philistines marks him as a king unprepared to face the enemy.

Saul seeks the ghostwife out of fear. After hearing Samuel's prediction of his death we are told, "And Saul hastened and flung himself full length on the ground and was very frightened by Samuel's words" (1, 28:20).

Saul's dread seems ever with him. When he is first anointed and summoned before the people we read, "They sought him but he was not to be found. And they inquired again of the Lord, 'Has a man come here?' And the Lord said, 'Look he is hidden among the gear'" (1, 10:22).

Saul's hiding not only symbolizes the anxiety at the core of his personality but reminds the reader of other biblical instances of hiding. In the Garden of Eden, Adam and Eve hide from shame. In the prophetic books hiding or avoiding God's call is a frequent trope. But as has wisely been said of Jonah, who literally tried to run away when God sent him to Nineveh to prophesy, he deserved to be a prophet because at least he tried to run from God only once. Saul will shirk his responsibility again and again. Hiding is a sign that an impressive exterior cannot mask internal hollowness and insecurity.

When Saul sins by keeping the best booty from the Amalekites and sparing the wicked king, his own explanation is that he listened to the people: "I have offended, for I have transgressed the utterance of the Lord, and your word, for I feared the troops and listened to their voice" (1, 15:24). Saul is frightened even of his own troops and unable to lead them.

Because of his inability to lead, Saul has barely skirted catastrophe earlier in his kingship. In a previous battle with the Philistines, Saul declares that any man who eats while the fighting rages shall be put to death. His own son Jonathan, not having heard the decree and having fought with exemplary bravery, reaches for some honey to revive himself and then is told of the vow. He objects on the ground that the troops need nourishment.

Saul discovers that Jonathan has indeed eaten in violation of his decree. He declares a death sentence on his own son: "So may God do to me, and even more, for Jonathan is doomed to die!" (1, 14:44). This same king has earlier refused to allow those who had challenged his rule to be put to death (1, 11). But now we begin to suspect that his magnanimity as well as his fierceness is a product of weakness, not strength.

Jonathan is saved by the voice of the people: "The troops said to Saul, 'Will Jonathan die, who has performed this great deliverance in Israel? Heaven forbid, as the Lord lives, that a single hair of his head should fall to the ground!'" (1, 14:45). Saul will save Jonathan *only* because of the voice of the people. When Jonathan later saves David from Saul's murderous rage, we can only wonder how much of his loyalty to David is motivated by memories of the day that his father was prepared to take his life in furtherance of a rash vow.

A hollow man is a poor trailblazer. Saul is the first king of Israel and in fairness has no precedent to follow. But even with the guidance of God and Samuel, God's priest and prophet, Saul requires his own vision and capacity and finds neither. Instead he seems captive to the people.

Samuel summarizes Saul's debility in a phrase that captures the paradox that will bring Saul down: "Though you may be small in your own eyes, you are the head of the tribes of Israel, and the Lord has anointed you king over Israel. And the Lord sent you on a mission . . . " (1, 15:17–18). Saul was chosen because of his stature and yet, as Samuel says, he is insignificant in his own eyes. His vengefulness against David is the reprisal of the small man, the one who deep down feels impotent to control the currents that surround him. Saul, king of Israel, cannot feel himself up to the enormous task, and his self-doubt ultimately destroys him.

In contrast to Saul's hiding among the gear, when Samuel first comes to anoint David, the lad is behind the house tending the sheep. He comes in readily and accepts the responsibility wordlessly.

Artfully drawing a contrast between Saul and David, the episode of Goliath sets the stage. This is one of three episodes that introduce David: First, we have seen him as the forgotten son, selected by Samuel, Israel's foremost religious authority. The distinction makes apparent that he is a special man. We then learn that David has the gentleness and musical skill to coax Saul from his melancholy. The third introduction, the story of Goliath, signals that this young man will not be another Saul. Saul does not understand the extent to which he, as king, must be unique. He lives in a universe where he is not the center. David is Ptolemaic. He knows that the world must revolve around him, second only to God. In a democracy that is a noxious philosophy, but in a theological monarchy, there is no room for a Copernican king.

David brims with self-assurance. He has an eye for the main chance (and the second and third chance, for that matter). He not only identifies the opportunity but assumes that he can accomplish what no one else in Israel would dare to do. Whatever the reason that Saul will not fight Goliath—his position as king or his usual anxiety—it hardly matters. The contrast is palpable and, for Saul, no doubt painful. Although David stands before Goliath and declares that he comes in the name of the Lord of Hosts, *God does not instruct him to take on the giant; David just knows instinctively that he should and that he can.* Whereas Saul disobeys God's will, David anticipates it. The qualities a reader will come to dislike or distrust about David, his audaciousness, his entitlement, are here on display in a way that makes it clear that he, and not Saul, must be king. His repeated escape from Saul emphasizes David's resourcefulness; that is the Goliath legacy. David's refusal to kill Saul when he can harks back to his sitting in the king's room strumming the lyre, underscoring the tenderness of the warrior. David is supremely inner-directed, in sociologist David Riesman's terminology; he is someone whose standards do not ultimately derive from the opinions of those around him.

When Saul first seeks to kill David, and throws a spear twice in an attempt to pin him to the wall, there is a remarkable sentence: "And David eluded him twice. And Saul was afraid of David" (1, 18:11–12). Saul has just tried to kill David, and it is Saul, not David, who is afraid. After the killing of the priests of Nob, when the sole survivor, Abiathar, on the run from Saul, finds his way to David, David's words—the words of this fugitive who is himself running for his life—are "Do not fear" (1, 22:23).

David is not recklessly daring. He does run from Saul, but that is simple self-preservation. In his fear of Achish, the Philistine king, and his maneuvering to save his own life, David shows that he can be productively cautious and wary. But the foundation of Saul's personality is fear. David, self-confident, quick-witted, gentle when needed, considerate with subordinates, and determinedly ruthless, is a king.

Still, we have seen that this king has one additional important and remarkable quality. David listens. The reader's first temptation is to assume that David is beloved in the manner of the classic narcissist—he incarnates the secret selfish wishes of others by being successful, and they love him for it. The narcissist is, in some way, what we wish we had the boldness to be. Yet David is the one who musically salves Saul's troubled spirit. A king is surrounded by self-absorbed toadies, but Saul loves David for being attuned to his sadness. David stands patiently while Abigail, talking about her husband, offers a long soliloquy, to which David responds showing that he has listened to her words. Most notably, later in the incident of Bathsheba and Uriah, David will listen to Nathan, not only to the parable but the conclusion and condemnation. David is receptive and sensitive. He may have used the priests of Nob to shelter and feed him, but when Saul has them killed, David blames himself for the part he played in their being singled out. David can be hard, but he is not one-dimensional; in the manner of a true leader he absorbs the concerns and states of others without being in thrall to them. Earlier we noted that the first utterance of a figure in the Bible matters: It is often significant in reading his or her character. David's first words ask what will be done for the one who strikes down Goliath. That suggests the grasping part of this ambitious man. But we should recall that there is an entire episode that precedes this, David's anointing. As Samuel summons and elevates him, David is silent. The capacity to be silent and receive, the ability to listen, are as crucial to David's leadership as his valor.

4

The King

SAUL'S DEMISE at the hands of the Philistines is a sad postscript to his gradual terrified fall. First his sons, including Jonathan, die in the battle. Saul is wounded by the Philistine archers
and asks his armor bearer to run him through with his sword.
When the soldier shrinks from regicide, Saul falls on his own
weapon and dies. The end is fitting for a King who destroyed
himself, abetted by an unsympathetic Samuel and an unrespon-
sive God.

The bodies of Saul and his sons are found by the Philistines, who dishonor the corpses, hanging them up for display.
The brave men of the town of Jabesh Gilead stage a nighttime
raid to recover the dismembered bodies, and bury the bones.

Now that Saul is gone David is surely king. There will be a
process of asserting David's rule over the northern part of the
country. Yet the man who preceded him, who feared him and who
threatened him, has been eliminated by the enemies of Israel.

David hears of Saul's death from an Amalekite who claims that the wounded king asked to be slain and that he himself obliged. He offers Saul's crown and armband to prove his case. David, who as a youngster shucked off the armor of Saul because it was too cumbersome, is now handed Saul's tokens of kingship. This time they have become his.

The Amalekite expects David to be pleased and to reward him for his mercy killing of David's enemy (which we know from the earlier account to be untrue in any case). David instead is incensed: "How were you not afraid to reach out your hand to do violence to the Lord's anointed?" (2, 1:14). David has the man killed, once again publicly disassociating himself from a death that was of profound benefit to him.

Sweet Singer of Israel

At the outset of our story, David's first public action was to sing away Saul's madness. His first public action as a king is to sing at Saul's death.

> The splendor, O Israel, on your heights lies slain,
> How the mighty have fallen . . . (2, 1:19)

David sings of how Saul clothed the women of Israel in scarlet and jeweled robes, and of Jonathan, whose "love was dearer to me than the love of women." The lament, full of expressively poignant lines—"Saul and Jonathan, beloved and dear in their life and their death they were not parted"—reminds us not only of David's capacity for grief but of his genius for expression.

At first it may seem strange to find an overflow of feeling in carefully crafted verses. In contrast to modern assumptions, however, emotional effusions in the ancient world fitted themselves into forms. Homer creates some of the most powerful scenes of literature, and some of the most heartrending speeches, in dactylic hexameters, and the lines are no less compelling for the strictness of the verse form. Spontaneous expression of feeling is not more authentic than carefully wrought words that give shape to grief and joy and yearning and faith. David does not suddenly break into poetry; first he mourns: "And they keened and they wept and they fasted till evening for Saul and for Jonathan his son and for the Lord's people and for the house of Israel for they had fallen by the sword" (2, 1:12). He has time to collect himself for the public presentation of his dirge.

Death was more present in the ancient world than in our own, but its incomprehensibility was, if anything, even greater than today. David has seen many people die. But Saul was a king, a father, a phantom, a pursuer. Saul's existence defined David's for many years. No matter how we construe David's relationship with Jonathan, there is no question that Saul's son loved David and saved his life. David's pain is heightened by the omission in the lament of any mention of afterlife or even of God. It is a moment of poetic desolation. David's life has been entwined with both men, and whatever relief he may justly feel at Saul's end is surely complicated and magnified by his new role and its responsibilities and perils. In losing Saul and Jonathan at once he is bereft of his nemesis/surrogate father and his friend. He has attained the summit, and from the heights intones his grief.

David's lament and his earlier musical service to Saul, alongside the poetry at the end of the book of Samuel, were determinative in the attribution of the Psalms to David. Not all are claimed by the Bible to be of Davidic authorship, and even the title "mizmor l'david" ("A psalm of David") can mean many things: a song to or about David as well as one *by* him. Yet the book of Psalms, the Psalter, has become bound up in the reading of his character throughout the ages.

The Talmud asks why David's authorship of Psalms was assumed and answers with a verse from the Song of Songs, attributed to David's son, Solomon: "Because his voice is sweet"

(Song of Sol. 2:14). David has the poetic gift and the struggling soul that generations of readers have found in the Psalms. In addition, throughout the Psalms we hear iterations of themes in David's life: pursuit by enemies, faith in God's deliverance, moments of despair, exultation, apprehension and the closeness of death. The Psalms pray for the peace of Jerusalem, plead with God to hear the Psalmist's voice and declare God's love. The Psalms fit David, his virtues, vicissitudes, cunning, and sins. Although many modern scholars assume the Psalms were actually written later than David, no matter the historical provenance, in a sacred book which features little in the way of individual prayer, the Psalms are the Bible's shining example of a single soul's devotional reach toward God. David is the first biblical protagonist drawn with all the colors of human character. We cannot know for sure that David gave birth to the Psalms, but we do know that for ages, readers of the Tanach have used the Psalms to have shape their understanding of the character of David.

In need of a capital to establish himself as king, David immediately asks guidance of God, who directs him to Hebron, in Judah. Judah, we recall, was the South, David's power base. There still exists opposition farther north. Ish-Bosheth, son of Saul, was not felled in battle, and he has joined forces with Abner, Saul's old commander. Abner served Ish-Bosheth the same way Joab served David. (Bosheth means "shame," an unlikely name and probably a denigrating play on words. His original name was probably Ish-Baal, Baal being a Canaanite god. Traces of idolatry were long lasting in Israel.)

So Abner and Ish-Bosheth wish to take the mantle of Saul and depose David. Following a skirmish with Joab and David's forces, Joab's brother, Asahel, runs after Abner to kill him. Abner is a skilled warrior; he does not wish to engage Joab's brother because, should he kill him, the professional enmity would turn personal and bitter. Abner tries to warn Asahel off to no avail.

Asahel keeps pursuing him. Spinning around in midchase, Abner skewers him. In a story about the perils and calculations of ambition, Asahel runs too fast. Joab and Abishai, the two remaining brothers, go off in pursuit of Abner.

There has been a great deal of bloodshed, and Abner has indeed killed in reluctant self-defense. So it is persuasive when Abner stands on top of the hill and offers a plaintive question to Joab: "Must the sword devour forever?" (2, 2:26). Joab stops, acquiesces, and goes home. But in his soul Joab is a man of the sword. He will not forget the death of his brother at Abner's hand.

Fighting between the house of Saul—Ish-Bosheth, Abner, and their troops—and the house of David, led by David and Joab, does not abate. Although David, with his base in the South, proves stronger, the northern forces are sufficient to prevent any final victory. As often happens in the story of David, it is a personal rather than a military incident that determines the outcome.

Abner and Ish-Bosheth, commander and leader, have a falling out over a concubine. Abner leaves in a huff and comes to David to switch allegiance. Since Abner still has power in the old house of Saul, David says that he will accept Abner to his side if the long-absent Michal, his former wife, is returned to him. The restoration is politically astute, as it signifies the unification of the houses of Saul and David. David's political position is fortified; he is reunited with Michal and linked to Abner —Saul's daughter and Saul's former commander have joined his side.

Sealing their alliance with a feast, David sends Abner off. Once again the political and personal intermingle. We recall that the Philistine commanders, long ago, did not trust David because he was an Israelite, no matter what allegiance he now claimed. Similarly, Joab, David's commander, does not trust an alliance with Abner, the former head of Saul's troops. Moreover, if Abner is the commander, where does that leave Joab, who until now has been David's uncontested military major domo? Most of all, Joab still hates Abner for having killed his brother Asahel, although the reader recalls that it was self-defense. It is therefore no surprise that Joab, after drawing Abner aside for a parlay, rams a dagger into his belly. "And he died for the blood of Asahel, Joab's brother" (2, 3:27). Abner is dead. Joab remains the commander of David's troops.

David immediately disclaims responsibility, "Innocent am I!" (2, 3:28). Once more we are presented with the startling scene of David's potential foes being dispatched without his participation or consent. Not only has Saul died, but so have all his sons who might contend for his throne save Ish-Bosheth, and David is not guilty of any of the slayings. For some readers the whiff of convenience has become the stench of conspiracy.

But it is too easy to continually cast the blame on David as though he secretly controlled all the currents swirling about him. The alliance with Abner, after all, can only have helped David, and Abner's murder by Joab is bound to reflect badly on David (David later exacts proxy revenge for this murder.) In the funhouse mirror of responsibility, where reflection doubles back on itself, David has a fair claim to guiltlessness. If all he wished to do was kill Abner, fighting against him when he was Saul's commander is a more plausible and straightforward strategy. To make an alliance with Abner and then have his commander Joab kill him is needlessly complex. David is not above subterfuge, but that does not mean that every seeming subterfuge is David's.

David leads the people in mourning for Abner and fasts for a day despite the desire of the people for him to eat. David again shows himself master of the public gesture: "And all the people took note and it was good in their eyes, all that the king had done was good in eyes of the people. And all the people and all Israel knew on that day that it had not been from the king to put to death Abner son of Ner" (2, 3:36–38). David will later fast for his sick child as a private person and we will see his heart; here he fasts as a king for a fallen enemy commander and we see his political skill.

What of Joab, the commander who killed Abner? David curses him for this slaying and orders him to tear his garment in mourning for Abner. Yet their collaboration continues unabated. There is some chance that this was a necessary, almost ritual humiliation, and that Joab, well acquainted with political realities, accepted it as the price of the assassination of Abner. More likely though, Joab, who has been largely responsible for David's ascendancy, while understanding the political necessities, resents the king's public rebuke. Pride is not always susceptible to reason, and Joab is a proud man. David disassociates himself from Joab's violent brothers—the sons of Zuriah—while calling himself a "gentle" man. This interplay of David's equanimity and ruthlessness, the man who plays the lyre and slays the giant, will serve him both well and ill in the time to come.

The death of Abner frightens Ish-Bosheth, the remaining claimant from the house of Saul. He has reigned in the North for two years. During that time the struggle has continued, with David's military gaining steadily. Saul has a grandson as well, Mephibosheth, son of Jonathan. But Mephibosheth is lame and not a candidate to rival David for kingship.

What does a reader suppose will happen to Ish-Bosheth? We know two things about David's enemies. First, they have an alarming tendency to die, whether from natural causes (Nabal) or by their own hands (Saul) or at the hands of someone David insists did not take orders from him (Abner). Second, we have seen that when murder takes place, David, in order to demonstrate his innocence, turns against the perpetrator of the deed, rebuking Joab and executing the man who claimed to have killed Saul. The one man who stands in the way of undisputed kingship for David is Ish-Bosheth. The smart money is on

Ish-Bosheth's lease on life being short—and that David will not be there when he meets his Maker.

And indeed, two men, Beerothites, a group of non-Israelites who had become absorbed into the tribe of Benjamin, sneak into Ish-Bosheth's bedchamber as he sleeps and kill him. Benjamin is Saul's tribe, so his son naturally lived in territory of Benjamin, where he might expect loyalty from the surrounding residents. The Beerothite assassins proudly bring Ish-Bosheth's head to David, demonstrating the peril of not reading the book in which you appear. Having dispatched David's rival to the throne, the killers assume he will reward them.

We know what David's response will be. If I killed the man who told me of Saul's death on the battlefield, David explains, how much more incensed must I be to be presented with the two of you, who have murdered an innocent man in his bed? David has them killed and dismembered, and buries Ish-Bosheth's head with Abner in Hebron.

In rapid succession we have seen the destruction of the house of Saul: The king and his sons have been killed in battle. Saul's chief commander, Abner, has been slain by Joab, presumably for personal vengeance. And now his remaining son who aspires to the throne, Ish-Bosheth, is killed by enterprising if misguided assassins. For each of these deaths David has plausible deniability. He did not hold the knife, and he has shown extravagant public displeasure with those who were responsible. Some scholars indict him, building the case that for each in the string of fortuitous deaths David has had a hand. Some of David's contemporaries clearly suspected the same, that he orchestrated the plot without leaving fingerprints. Did David feed the Philistines intelligence during the battle that killed Saul? We know of his association with the Philistine king Achish, who wanted him to participate in that very battle. Did David really want Abner gone and give Joab a secret wink and a nod? Were the Beerothites who killed Ish-Bosheth expecting a reward because they acted on David's implicit or explicit orders?

The Tanach goes to a great deal of trouble to insist that David was blameless. For many modern scholars this is an indication that it was written by partisans of David's "house"—that is, the kings of Judah who came from the Davidic line. They were whitewashing the founder and thereby granting greater legitimacy to the royal descendants. Still, the attempt to turn David into a Machiavellian thoroughbred does violence to the complexity of his character. There are shades of David's soul we have not yet seen.

With the death of Ish-Bosheth, David is now the king of both Judah and Israel. He must consolidate his reign by founding a capital city, subduing the enemies of Israel, and establishing his house, both literal and governmental.

"And all the elders of Israel came to the king in Hebron, and King David made a pact with them in Hebron before the Lord, and they anointed David as king over Israel. Thirty years old was David when he became king, forty years he was king" (2, 5:3–4). Saul had been king in Gibeah, in the area of Benjamin. His son Ish-Bosheth had transferred his kingship to the city of Jabesh Gilead, both farther north and east across the Jordan. Ish-Bosheth's choice had the benefit of being more remote from David's southern center of power. Now there is one king for all. The North-South split, briefly healed under David and Solomon, will reassert itself after Solomon's death until the North is conquered by the Assyrians in the eighth century, scattering the "ten lost tribes."

David has reigned in Hebron, in the South. Although in retrospect the transfer of the capital to Jerusalem seems obvious, at the time Jerusalem was a tiny backwater whose strategic advantages could be discerned only by a military/political leader of greatness. Jerusalem belonged to neither North nor South. As many have pointed out, the city's geography made it a sort of Washington, D.C., that could serve as the ideal capital for the king of a unified Judah and Israel.

Notwithstanding the frequency with which it has been conquered over the centuries, Jerusalem is a difficult city to capture. The surrounding hills make for ready defense. Long before David, the book of Joshua had recorded failure to take Jerusalem: "And as for the Jebusites, inhabitants of Jerusalem, the children of Judah could not drive them out" (Joshua 15:63). The Bible recounts that even Nebuchadnezzar, king of mighty Babylonia, managed to overcome the city only after a prolonged siege (2 Kings 25:1–10).

David takes Jerusalem easily. The method, however, is unknown. Chronicles gives credit to Joab (1 Chron. 11:6: "Joab, son of Zeruiah attacked first"). There have been speculations, based in part on contested translations, of darting raids in shafts and water pipes. Experts cannot be sure. Through some combination of daring, luck, and God's favor, Jerusalem was taken, and "The City of David"—the King's chosen capital—established.

Attention now turns to David's vexed relationship with the Philistines. The Philistines were Israel's constant foe in biblical times. David, having taken refuge in their territory when pursued by Saul, now turns on his old protectors. The battle in which Saul and his sons died gave the Philistines control over the center of the country. David asks God (presumably through the urim and thummim, as before) whether he should march against the Philistines, and God assures him of victory. God even instructs David on battle tactics, seeming to suggest that David attack from behind, which ultimately proves successful. The Philistines are not gone, but they no longer pose a threat to the contiguous rule of David over Israel and Judah. Although the battles do not occupy a great deal of the narrative, subduing the Philistine threat is a signal accomplishment of David's reign.

At this point, almost in passing, the text mentions that David takes more wives and concubines, siring more sons and daughters. David is more and more the picture of a successful king, and he now turns to honor the God who first promised and now has enabled his triumph.

The ark of the covenant is the central symbol of Israelite faith. It has a peripatetic history: Carried by the Israelites through the desert, it finally comes to Israel. At different times the ark moves to Gilgal, comes to rest in Shiloh, is captured and then returned by the Philistines, and passes through Beth Shemesh. At this moment in our story it rests at Kirjath Jearim. There it has stayed until David resolves to bring it to his capital. God's presence as symbolized by the tablets in the ark will be a continuing assurance that David's leadership will be blessed.

Once David recovers the ark and celebrates its restoration, the pageant on the way to the capital is struck by a mysterious and disturbing calamity. One of the oxen pulling the cart that bears the ark stumbles and a man named Uzzah, fearing for the ark, reaches out and holds it to ensure it does not fall. Instantly God strikes him down.

What do we make of this story? Some have attributed it to the incorrect means of transporting the ark—it should be carried by poles on the affixed rings and on the shoulders of the Levites, not loose in a wagon (cf. Num. 7:9). Others see the ark as a box charged with divine energy that cannot be touched. Still others see this as an example of the titanic peevishness of a God who slays at whim.

Theologically, we can take note of the insight of Rav Kook, twentieth-century scholar and mystic, who pointed out that it was the oxen that stumbled. Uzzah should have steadied the animals, not the ark. Kook sees this as a paradigm of those who seek to change God's word to suit the challenges of the world instead of seeking to right the problems in accord with the law. However homiletic, Kook's interpretation is one more indication of the profoundly mysterious, troubling nature of the episode.

David's reaction, however, is clear and immediate. Both

angry and fearful, he no longer wishes the ark to reside in the city. Perhaps he reads this as a withdrawal of divine favor from him. So the ark is placed in the house of one Obed-edom the Gittite. Obed-edom and his house begin to thrive. When told that the "Ark blessed" Obed-edom and his house, David resolves anew to bring it to the City of David, "with rejoicing."

David arranges an extravagant procession. His wife Michal, whom he has forcibly retrieved from Paltiel, sees him dancing and is disgusted by the spectacle. In addition to her natural bitterness at being shuffled around at the caprice of powerful men, she must wonder at the series of deaths that have befallen the house of Saul. Now she quarrels with David, sarcastically commenting: "How honored today is the king of Israel who has exposed himself today to the eyes of his servants' slavegirls as some scurrilous fellow would expose himself!" (2, 6:20). As noted above, the concluding words of the chapter are "And Michal daughter of Saul had no child till her dying day" (2, 6:23). The kingship will never be of Saul's lineage.

Once the ark has returned, governmental and sacramental leadership fuse, giving David the status not only of king but of the anointed one of God, who has established the sacred center of God's people.

When the book of Samuel began, the priest was the central figure in Israel. Increasingly, power and sanctity are attributes of the king. The move from priesthood to kingship is echoed in many ancient civilizations. Choosing a king is a way of declaring oneself a people. In Judges, the biblical book preceding Samuel, we are told that "there was no king in Israel" (Judg. 19:1; 21:25) and that "all the people did what was right in their own eyes" (21:25).

Religious authorities do not yield easily, however, and they distrust the growth of secular power. The Tanach struggles with the concept of kingship. Alongside the priest and prophet, the king must serve a function of leadership without tyranny.

In Deuteronomy the people are warned that a king must not accumulate too many wives or great riches, or send back to Egypt for horses—in short, a king should still be subordinate to God the King. To help ensure this, a king must write his own copy of the Torah (Deut. 17:15–19). In literally writing down the regulations of the Torah, he is expected to internalize the restraints on his own power. Other passages are more minatory; Samuel, no doubt personally threatened as well as theologically discomfited, made it clear to the people what a demand for a king would mean:

> This will be the practice of the king who will reign over you. Your sons he will take and set for himself in his chariots and in his cavalry, and some will run before his chariots. He will set for himself captains of thousands and captains of fifties, to plow his ground and reap his harvest and to make his implements of war and the implements of his chariots. And your daughters he will take as confectioners and cooks and bakers. . . . And you will cry out on that day before your king whom you chose for yourselves and he will not answer you on that day. (1, 8:11–18)

Scholar Michael Walzer identifies three distinct but intermingling conceptions of kingship in Israel. There is the view above, which sees monarchy as a rejection of theocracy. Under God's rule a king should not be necessary. The second, which we find in the Psalms, sees the king as God's covenantal partner, and in some ways subsuming the identity of the people into the kingship. The third is a compromise between the two, approved by God but mainly concerned with the pragmatics of rule. Yair Lorberbaum puts it similarly: "Direct theocracy (in which the king is God) and royal theology (in which God is king) and limited monarchy (the king is not God)."

David is now in the process of defining where he will be on that continuum. Although anointed by Samuel, reassured by

God and interacting with both priests and prophets, David has only now arrived as the acknowledged king of God's people. With the ark symbolically in place, it is time to take the further step, attested to in both the ancient and modern worlds: God must have a dwelling place on earth. David will build a Temple. His resolve is commemorated in Psalm 132: "O Lord, remember in David's favor his extreme self-denial / how he swore to the Lord. . . . I will not give sleep to my eyes, or slumber to my eyelids / until I find a place for the Lord . . . " (Ps. 132:1–5).

The language and tenor of 1 Samuel undergo an abrupt change at this moment. Shifting from narrative to theology, both God (through the prophet Nathan) and David offer extended speeches. They are intended to establish the permanence of the Davidic dynasty. Despite all that will happen, both to David and his successors, embedded in this seventh chapter of the second book of Samuel is the promise that will later cheer generations of Jews who will wander, dispossessed. No matter David's other, less exalted actions and words, the resolve to build a Temple for God, so crucial to Israel's later history, will enshrine him forever as a leader cherished in Israel's memory.

David summons the prophet Nathan. The king is struck by an apparent imbalance in his accommodations and those of the ark of God; why should a human monarch have a palace and God have no dedicated home in Israel? He says to Nathan, "See, pray, I dwell in a cedarwood house while the Ark of God dwells within curtains" (2, 7:2). Nathan, at first, approves of David's plan to build a Temple, but later God comes to him in a night vision. No, David will not build a house for God. God insists that He has never dwelt in a house, that instead of receiving a gift God will promise: that Israel will rest easy and no more be afflicted. Rather than David raising a house for God, Nathan explains, "The Lord declares that it is He who will make you a house" (2, 7:11).

What follows is the most comprehensive promise granted

to any character in the Bible. However David has achieved his status, God declares him worthy and his rule enduring. The "house" moves from literal to metaphorical—the house of David will endure. David is also promised that his son and successor will indeed build a Temple for God: "He it is who will build a house for My name and I will make the throne of his kingship unshaken forever. I will be a father to him and he will be a son to me, so should he do wrong, I will chastise him with the rod men use and with the afflictions of humankind. But My loyalty shall not swerve from him as I made it swerve from Saul whom I removed before you. And your house and your kingship shall be steadfast forever, your throne unshaken forever" (2, 7:13–16).

David is assured that what happened with Saul will not recur; God will not withdraw His favor. David responds by declaring his unworthiness and his gratitude, then reiterates the promise, as if nailing it down in perpetuity: "For You, O Lord of Hosts, God of Israel, have revealed to Your servant, saying, 'A house I will build you.' Therefore has Your servant found the heart to pray to you this prayer. And now, O Lord God, You are God and Your words must be truth, You have spoken this bounty to Your servant. And now, have the goodness to bless the house of Your servant to be before you forever, for it is you, Lord God, Who have spoken . . . " (2, 7:27–29).

Why does God refuse David's request to build the Temple? According to the book of Samuel, God does not need a Temple. Nathan tells David in God's name, never has a previous leader of Israel been reproached for not building a home for the God of all the world. All this is convincing, but if so, why does God assure him that Solomon will do it? In a parallel story in Chronicles (1, 22:7–8), David reports to Solomon that God decided David shed too much blood in warfare. Chronicles makes it a moral issue—the warrior should not build God's home. In a pragmatic sense, too, the prevalence of battle in David's life may well explain why he did not build the Temple.

John Adams wrote to his wife in 1780, "I must study Politicks and War that my sons may have liberty to study Mathematicks and Philosophy." Similarly, David may have been too preoccupied establishing and then maintaining his kingship to have the leisure for grand building projects. He was the pioneer and Solomon the settler.

Solomon, having inherited a more peaceful kingdom, was able to follow the usual practice in the ancient world of building a Temple in gratitude and tribute to God who maintained him on the throne. Poet Theodore Roethke's line applies: "A house for wisdom: a field for revelation." David the shepherd found God, and Solomon's domesticated life enshrined God. Later, in a message to King Hiram of Tyre that summarizes both views, Solomon will write, "You know that my father David could not build a house for the name of the Lord his God because of the war that surrounded him" (1 Kings 5:17). The child will complete the paternal project. Solomon's words to Hiram call to mind Carl Jung's observation that the greatest influence on the lives of children is the unlived lives of their parents.

In the context of "power balance" between David and God, the refusal to let David build the Temple makes sense. David has survived and is king. He is deeply indebted to God. To build a Temple would, in some sense, put God in his debt. It would change the relationship between them. Solomon is entirely different. His Temple is an expression of the solidity of the kingdom and the completion of a project of his father's. For David the drive to build is a wish to give God something that David already has—a house. God will not take from the man whom He has made king. In the dialogue that takes place, God reverses the proposal, saying essentially, you think you will make a house for Me? Indeed, I will make one for you. The balance is restored.

Psalm 89, often taken to be a commentary on God's promises to David, begins, "I will sing of the Lord's steadfast and eternal love/to all the generations my lips will declare your faithfulness. I declare, 'Your enduring love is established forever'" (Ps. 90:2–3). For this moment God and David are in harmony.

This is the zenith of David's kingship. He rules justly and his children serve as priests, pointing to influence over both the sacramental and political branches of state. Secure, David is moved to magnanimity. He seeks any surviving members of Saul's house with whom he can keep faith "for the sake of Jonathan." (Later several men of the house of Saul are executed, which leads some to think that these events are chronologically out of sync.) Jonathan has a surviving, lame son named Mephibosheth. David summons him and gives him a place at his table. His lame status reminds us of the decline of Saul's fortunes compared with those of David, who came to Jerusalem leaping and dancing before the ark. It also reinforces the idea that he can pose no dynastic threat. Some commentators see a sinister cast to David's bringing Mephibosheth to him, as though it were more house arrest than home hospitality. But there seems no compelling reason to impute malign motives to David's welcome of Mephibosheth. It is a relatively cost-free kindness and is no doubt looked upon with favor by his own circle.

First observed in road-safety experiments, there is a psychological principle often called "risk compensation." When people feel safe, they will act in riskier ways. You may drive faster wearing a seat belt than unbuckled. The presence of a lifeguard leads swimmers to try deeper waters. So there is a certain emotional logic that shortly after God has assured David of his everlasting protection, things begin to fall apart. Now that David is triumphant in battle, secure in his kingship, beloved of God and heralded by the people, is there not, as in Greek tragedy, the almost certain presumption of fall? Security slides into complacency; knowing the permanence of his dynasty reduces his vigilance. Perhaps it would have happened in any case. Surely David's life was never governed by a principle of prudence, no matter how safe he felt.

5

The Sinner

Weaknesses do not arrive singly. Like strengths, they are clustered, and each weakness interlocks with other failings in the structure of our personalities. In public life, when some sin or crime is exacerbated by the cover-up, we learn anew that faults seek the shade of others like themselves; all yearn for the company of kindred—even character traits.

So as we unspool the saga of Bathsheba, where one transgression leads on to ever greater ones, it should not amaze us that it was so difficult for a man like David to stop with a single sin. Inertia is a law of spiritual life as it is of physical life. The Rabbis understood our tendencies well when they said in the Talmud, "One is led in the direction one wishes to go" (Makkot 10b).

David is a secure king when the episode of Bathsheba begins. The classical translation of 2, 11:1 is "In spring, the time when kings go to war." A more literal translation has it "At the turn of the year, the time when kings go to war." The import is that when the skies clear and the ground hardens, when fighting is promising and possible, nations prepare their armies and the kings go forth. Rashi comments that the fields are full of stalks of grain for horses to eat. The same sense of anticipation, even festivity, attaches to a season for gaming or mating. War was a diversion, a mission, and a sport all at once. But already there is something amiss in Israel:

> And it happened at the turn of the year, at the time kings sally forth, that David sent out Joab and his servants with him and all Israel, and they ravaged the Ammonites and besieged Rabbah. And David was sitting in Jerusalem. (2, 11:1)

The verse hints at the upheaval to come. Now is the time when *kings* go to war, but David does not go. The troops sally forth and succeed without him. And should we for a moment misunderstand the import of David's *sending* Joab, the Bible reiterates that David sat in Jerusalem. It does not say "sat smugly in Jerusalem," but we may well read the adverb into the verse.

Saul and Jonathan have died and David is the undisputed king. He is not without enemies and opposition. In the previous chapter the Ammonites insult David's messengers, leading to a war in which Israel routs the opposition. There are those in Israel who seemingly await the chance to express their solidarity with the house of Saul. Still, for now David is the secure sovereign of all Israel.

He has proposed building a house for God, but God has proposed instead to build a house for David, an everlasting kingship. In short, this upstart, this once neglected child, has accumulated power and women and a divine promise greater than any before him. Perhaps he stays behind in Jerusalem because daring has given way to wonder at the prosperity that he does not wish to risk in war. Perhaps he wants to run his good fortune through his fingers like the gold coins of legend.

Or it may be that David suffers from the vertigo of success.

To have risen so quickly, to be God's chosen one, beloved of the people, powerful and young, with fistfuls of promise, may require a balance, a leveling. A fall.

David rises from his house and walks about on the roof, "And he saw from the roof a woman bathing, and the woman was very beautiful." David inquires and is told she is "Bathsheba daughter of Eliam wife of Uriah the Hittite" (2, 11:2–3). The double identification reinforces how much she cannot belong to David. She is a woman with both a husband and a father. She is under the care and protection of others. Hands off.

> And David sent messengers and fetched her and she came to him and he lay with her. (2, 11:4)

Unlike the relationship with Michal and Abigail, where the women chose David, here David is the active principal. He pursues Bathsheba. This first half of this verse is imagined by Rembrandt's Bathsheba. She is summoned: Bathsheba sits looking down, somewhat sadly, with a note in her hand. The reader knows that this note, summoning her to the palace, will carry in its wake a host of implications for the bearer, the writer, and all of Israel. In the artist's usual fashion, Bathsheba is lit against a dark background, carrying some theological weight. What is about to happen is criminal and dark. In the end, however, the result will be the birth of a new ruler of Israel.

A sordid interlude becomes a historic tragedy. After her rendezvous at the palace, Bathsheba returns home but soon informs the king that she is pregnant. Her husband is off at war—David's war with Ammon—and too many people surround the king to keep a secret. When the child becomes evident, so will David's transgression.

Now one weakness begets another and another. David asks Joab, the head of his military, to send Uriah home to him. When Uriah arrives, David tells him to go home and "bathe your feet." That could be simple traveling advice or a metaphor for sex. Of course it may also be a slight eruption from David's subconscious, since he has seen Uriah's wife bathing. In any case, he has not reckoned with the nobility of the husband of this beautiful woman. When Uriah refuses to go to his home and is asked why, he responds:

> The ark and Israel and Judah are sitting in huts, and my master Joab and my master's servants encamped in open fields, and shall I then come to my house to eat and to drink and to lie with my wife? By your life, by your very life, I will not do this thing. (1, 11:11)

The power of Uriah's righteousness—Uriah, recall, is identified as a Hittite, not an Israelite—stands in painful, poignant contrast to David's perfidy. The contrast grows more vivid. Increasingly desperate, David gets Uriah drunk. In addition to David's scheming, his cynical view of human nature is apparent: He believes that nobility is a facade that can be shattered. A few drinks and David will have his way. After all, if David could spot Bathsheba from the roof, Uriah's house must be close by. To David, for whom lust had proved irresistible, the temptation to make the short trip would seem overwhelming. But Uriah, drunk and long chaste, still refuses to go to his wife while his comrades are fighting in the field. David is defeated by the rectitude of the very man he betrayed.

But he can sink lower still. In a maneuver of breathtaking hauteur and cruelty, David asks Uriah himself to deliver a letter to his general Joab—without knowing that it carries Uriah's own death sentence. The letter reads "Put Uriah in the face of the fiercest battling and draw back, so that he will be struck down and die" (1, 11:15).

Uriah's death will not solve David's problem. David will still be exposed as an adulterer by the timing of the birth. Yet we will see that David's conscience, here as in the future, often salves itself by ruthlessness. Rather than face Uriah every day, a living reminder of his deed, he will marry Bathsheba. David's sense of entitlement has grown so great that he wishes not only to sin, but to do so with a clear conscience.

Honorable to the end, Uriah delivers the letter to Joab, who follows orders. Joab sends back a messenger with report of the battle. The report includes several who died in the battle. Joab, pragmatic in protecting his king, knows that he cannot consign Uriah alone to death without arousing suspicion, so he places others in jeopardy as well. No doubt David will at first be vexed that other soldiers perished. Joab tells the messenger that if David disapproves of any tactics or results, simply end the report with, "Your servant Uriah also died."

The servant duly reports and David, signaling his satisfaction, sends a message in return: "Thus shall you say to Joab, 'Let this thing not seem evil in your eyes, for the sword devours sometimes one way and sometimes another. Battle all the more fiercely against the city and destroy it.' And so rouse his spirits" (1, 11:25). David's message to Joab, serene and cheering, is a code of congratulations for conspiracy. But even a king of Israel cannot change the reality of the moral order: For two verses after David says "Let this thing not seem evil" we are told, "the thing that David had done was evil in the eyes of the Lord" (1, 11:27). After Bathsheba's period of mourning for her husband, David summons her and she becomes his wife and she bears him a son.

The cover-up in this case was surely worse than the crime. Adultery is less grievous than premeditated murder. The first is a sin of impulse, the second cold and deliberate. Until this moment David has guarded his reputation zealously. As we shall see later when recounting his life as a brigand, a warrior, and a captain, when David's enemies are vanquished, he is always careful to provide himself a more or less plausible alibi. When he had the chance to take Saul's life, he did not, in part because of affection and awe, and in part because he knew the stain on his reputation would be indelible.

Cover-ups are about the danger of people discovering who you really are or what you have really done. They are about avoiding public shame and distrusting in the forgiveness of others or the resilience of oneself. David, for all his strength, has a certain lack of faith, or betrays some hollowness at his core. He cannot have his deed known: What would the troops, Uriah, his wives, the people say? One wonders whether in some corner there is a fancy that he can keep God from knowing if he can hide it from everyone else. For unlike in other moments, David does not pray. The psalm associated with Bathsheba, Psalm 51, is a plea set after the prophet Nathan approaches him accusingly. First David feels the slightly-uneasy-but-exhilarated sense of a man who has sinned and gotten away with it.

What of Bathsheba? Could she have refused David? Throughout the generations Bathsheba has been portrayed as both vixen and victim. Why was she bathing on the roof? Was it to catch the attention of the king or just her normal bathing ritual? Did she jump at David's summons or feel that she had no choice, a vulnerable woman whose husband was away? Since Bathsheba herself is silent throughout the episode, save for announcing her pregnancy, we will never know. Much later on in David's story, at the end of his life, Bathsheba will play a significant role. But we cannot judge her acquiescence here, a young married woman summoned by the king, by her bearing after years of living as David's wife. Bathsheba is one of the Bible's great Rorschach tests, like Job's wife. Our view of her says more about us than it does about her.

Was David taken more by lust or by love? His willingness to recall Uriah from the battlefield and send him home drunk suggests more a postcoital panic than a consuming love. Grand passion though it may have been, it was not the type to sweep all calculation aside. The murder of Uriah necessitated marriage; had Uriah been less honorable, it is not at all clear that David and Bathsheba would have seen each other again.

Of course, cover-ups are futile before an omniscient God. In ancient Israel, God spoke primarily through prophets. There were even bands and schools of prophets, chosen for their gifts and trained. As with priests and warriors, prophets formed an indispensable part of the retinue of rulers. Although we know little about the prophet Nathan, in the time of David he was clearly a formidable force. Samuel tells us that God sent him to David. Nathan tells the following parable:

> Two men there were in a single town, one was rich and the other poor. The rich man had sheep and cattle, in great abundance. And the poor man had nothing save one little ewe that he had bought. And he nurtured her and raised her with him together with his sons. From his crust she would eat and from his cup she would drink and in his lap she would lie and she was to him like a daughter. And a wayfarer came to the rich man, and it seemed a pity to him to take from his own sheep and cattle to prepare for the traveler who had come to him, and he took the poor man's ewe and prepared it for the man who had come to him. (2, 12:1–4)

David's reaction is instantaneous and violent. "As the Lord lives, doomed is the man who has done this!" Some read this as an actual death verdict, others as a moral condemnation, that such a man would deserve death. Then David continues: "And the poor man's ewe he shall pay back fourfold, in as much as he has done this thing, and because he had no pity" (2, 12:5–6).

"And Nathan said to David: 'You are the man.'"

Behold a hinge of history. No matter how literally we take the story of David, this moment of reaction is indelible and enduring. Nathan continues to speak in God's voice, telling David that he has given him everything, and would have given more, but David instead chose to commit both adultery and murder "by the sword of the Ammonites"—reminding us of the special cowardice involved in proxy murder. As a result, the son born of the adulterous union will die and another will lie with David's wives.

Here is what David did not do: He did not have Nathan put to death.

Medieval history is dominated by the theme of power struggles between the church and the state. But we do not see Nathan reaching for power. His is not a sacramental or priestly role, it is the role of the prophet. The parable is the thing by which he will stir the conscience of the king. Note how well wrought is Nathan's strategy. By beginning the story with a tale of injustice, he has allowed David to render judgment before confronting him with his own evil. He has given David space to be good, to morally reorient himself. He persuades David to be the righteous king, and when David is in that frame of mind, accuses him of being heinously wicked. In the Talmud, there is a term, "raminhu"—literally, "he throws him against himself" —to describe one's own words used against oneself. Nathan does that to David, with stunning effect.

David's reaction of immediate penitence—"I have offended against the Lord"—reminds us that piety can coexist in a soul with myriad other qualities, enviable and base. Might David have sought to quiet Nathan? In the history of monarchy the voice of rebuke is generally not tolerated (one is reminded of the moral minuet of Henry II and Becket). Cultures from which Israel took its models of kingship are reflected in the story the Greek historian Herodotus tells of Cambyses, the Persian king who reigned some five hundred years after David. Cambyses wanted to marry his sister, forbidden in Persian law, and summoned counselors to advise him. They prudently reported that while they could find no law permitting the king to marry his sister, they did discover laws that permitted the king to do whatever he wished. So fortified, Cambyses married.

Could David do whatever he wished? As recounted above, Saul embarked on a wholesale slaughter of the priests of Nob. If a king could with impunity kill an assemblage of priests, surely the king could dispatch one troublesome prophet. In later generations not only will the pagan Queen Jezebel seek the life of Elijah (1 Kings 19), but the Israelites of Anathot will seek to kill the prophet Jeremiah when they dislike his message (Jer. 11). Prophets were not exempt from persecution. That David did not seek to silence Nathan might be, religiously and historically, his moment of redemption.

Nathan's parable itself also contains a reminder to David. Recall that when David fled, Saul gave Michal, David's wife and Saul's daughter, to Paltiel. So David, who was at that time a young, frightened fugitive, knows what it is to lose "the single lamb." When Nathan says, "You are the man," he does not specify which man. It is consistent with David's life that he is everyman in the parable: rich, poor, victim, and thief. In a subtle masterstroke, Nathan even uses the same Hebrew word, "rash," that David used to refer to himself when Saul offered to marry David to his daughter (1, 18:23). But in the Hebrew text of Nathan's speech an aleph is added, so the word "rash," meaning poor, is spelled like "rosh," meaning head—or king. David is both poor and royal, the prodigy who rose and the star who fell.

Bathsheba gives birth to a son. The child falls sick and David fasts in the hope of saving the boy's life. In desperation and fear he spends the night "lying on the ground" (2, 12:16) just as he "lies" with Bathsheba, Uriah refuses to "lie" with his wife, and Nathan warns David that another man will, in punishment, "lie" with his women, a prophecy that will come to pass later with the rebellion of Absalom. The recurrence of the word "lie"—what Buber and Rosenzweig in their German translations of the Bible called the leitworts that thread through the biblical narratives—reminds us that the same word can, as commentator Phyllis Trible writes, take a "pilgrimage." Words change their nuances as we move from neutral use to tension to tragedy.

Modern English translator Everett Fox points out that "send" has a similarly powerful trail in this story. Eleven times in these twenty-six verses messages and people are sent, almost always by David. David sends for Bathsheba, for Uriah, and sends a message to Joab. Each sending increases the foreboding until the culminating moment when God *sends* Nathan.

David fasts and prays. On the seventh day the child dies, and David's servants fear telling him, for they have seen his distress while hoping for the child's survival. But David confounds their expectations. He sees them whispering and asks, "Is the child dead?" When they confirm the death, he rises, bathes, prays, and asks for food.

The servants are perplexed: "What is this thing you have done? For the sake of the living child you fasted and wept, and when the child was dead, you arose and ate food?" David answers, "While the child was still alive I fasted and wept, for I thought, 'Who knows, the Lord may favor me and the child will live.' And now that he is dead, why should I fast? Can I bring him back again? I am going to him and he will not come back to me" (2, 12:22–23).

What does this counterintuitive, if logical, reaction tell us about David? Is he a romantic or a ruthless pragmatist? Here his definition of prayer is instrumental: He does not pray to pour out his heart, express his contrition or distress, but to win God's favor. True, Psalm 51 gives a somewhat different picture, but even there, he expresses (as he does to Nathan) that his sin is against God ("Against you alone have I sinned" [51:6]). Surely he has sinned against Uriah and Bathsheba and the nation of Israel, but that is not the focus of his contrition. He aims his sorrow at the One with power to change its consequences.

Perhaps in David's mind his prayer for seven days fulfilled the customary period of mourning. Perhaps the circumstances were known and he felt uneasy publicly mourning for the child of his adultery. Or it may be, as some have speculated, that in an age of frequent infant death, mourning for a child shortly after birth was curtailed. Swedish novelist Torgny Lindgren's

Bathsheba captures the pathos in the infant's passing: "His eyes do not need to be closed, since he has never opened them."

We know that the repercussions have not ended, for Nathan's words to David during their encounter will echo: "I am about to raise up evil against you from your own house" (1, 12:11) in the later rebellion of David's son Absalom.

David's reaction in the wake of the child's death offers insights into the dynamics of David's character. One of the recurring questions of David's life is "Does David love?" D. H. Lawrence, for example, in an early and little known work, *David: A Play*, describes David's relationships with Saul's house with the same perfervid eloquence that characterizes his novels: Michal asks, "Why do you not love me and never care?" and David responds, "It is not in me. I have been blithe of thy love and thy body." As he runs from the house, he assures her: "Thou shalt not weep for me, for thou are a delight to me, even a delight and a forgetting."

A reader goes searching for clues to David's true emotional composition in his relationships with Jonathan, with Michal, with Abigail, with Bathsheba, and with his children. The question will arise anew in regard to his firstborn, Amnon, and David's shattering reaction to the end of Absalom's revolt. As my brother Paul, who teaches sociology at Emory, pointed out to me, David's descent from Ruth—since the book of Ruth is essentially a love story—suggests at least there is love in his lineage. One brief, tender scene in the aftermath of his child's death hints at a genuine empathy in David:

> And David consoled Bathsheba his wife, and he came to her and lay with her, and she bore a son and called his name Solomon, and the Lord loved him. (2, 12:24)

Only now, after the death of the child, is Bathsheba called David's wife. (The Talmud calls David and Bathsheba "soulmates" [San. 107a].)

Although his fate will not be realized for decades, there is an intimation in "and the Lord loved him" that Solomon will be king after David, as indeed comes to pass. The name Solomon, most scholars believe, means "replacement." Whether a replacement for Uriah or, more plausibly, for Bathsheba's first child, we cannot know. The name itself permits us a glimpse into Bathsheba's mind, but it is still opaque: If Solomon is the replacement for her first child, is Uriah therefore forgotten or is he irreplaceable? If Solomon is the replacement for Uriah, is the first child forgotten? How did David console Bathsheba over the death of the child whose existence led her present husband to kill her former one? We know that Bathsheba will become the fierce advocate of her son Solomon, maneuvering toward the end of David's life to ensure Solomon's succession. Does she come to love the man she is now tied to for life and throughout the annals of history? Michal and Jonathan are said to love David, but such a phrase is never used to describe Bathsheba's feelings toward him. They have share much—more, in some ways, than human beings should shared. David has committed terrible wrongs, although Bathsheba may conclude that he did so out of passion for her. We do know, if we know anything about David, that for all his flaws, he was easy to love.

The story of David and Bathsheba precedes a series of disastrous events in the life of David and Israel. Some scholars believe it was placed deliberately in the text at this point not for chronological purposes but to outline a moral arc to the tale. Others believe the point of the story was to prove the legitimacy of Solomon, that he was unarguably David's son. In judging the placement and authorship of stories, scholars rely upon several strands: language, names, references that suggest both order and feel of a narrative. For some, the Bathsheba story is a radical break with what went before and also what comes after. Previously David has always been provided with a plausible reason for his conduct. Here is an egregious sin and a coldblooded assassination of his own soldier, Uriah. Of course, consistency in character is necessary in fiction for plausibility, but in life we routinely discover that we do things "unlike" ourselves.

Why *would* David do such a thing? We can imagine the internal rationalizations of a king who knows that many of his troops will inevitably die in war, that they are in his service after all, and that the greater good of Israel is served by his leadership. What Nathan punctures in parable is not only David's dormant conscience but his self-deceptions and rationalizations.

Traditional commentators are agonizingly uncomfortable with the story. First, the Talmud seeks to exonerate David of adultery with Bathsheba by insisting that soldiers going off to war gave their wives a "get," a bill of divorce. Should a soldier not return and be unaccounted for, his wife would not be tied to him and unable to remarry. Technically, the Talmud therefore insists, Bathsheba was divorced from Uriah when David took her for himself. And in the most transparent attempt to get David off the moral hook, some ancient rabbis insisted that, as Uriah disobeys the king who instructs him to go home to his wife, he proves his primary loyalty to Joab and not to David, since Uriah cites his inability to go home when "my master Joab and my master's servants (are) encamped in open fields . . . " (2, 11:11). Through that disobedience, Uriah is guilty of treason and therefore liable to death. Such contortions come from a refusal to face deep divisions in our heroes. The Bible actually leaves us little room to exonerate David. The medieval commentator Abravanel lists five separate major sins committed by David: adultery; an attempt to distort the lineage of a child; the death of Uriah and the collateral deaths and injuries as a result of that maneuver; robbing Uriah of the dignity of death on his own land and ensuring that he is killed by an enemy of Israel; and marrying Bathsheba, in an apparent lack of remorse. Only his subsequent repentance, Abravanel concludes, redeems David in God's eyes.

Tracing David's internal strife, his kaleidoscopic emotions, may seem a product of modern sensibilities. Yet since he is king and his relationships are decisive for the course of his rule, understanding David necessitates constantly recalibrating his volatile soul. The emotional tremors of this single man alter the subsequent history of all Israel. His strengths will establish the kingdom on a new foundation, and his weaknesses leave enduring cracks.

As is so often the case, nothing will showcase vulnerabilities like a child. The longest single episode in the story of David is also the one that crystallizes his intertwined capacities and flaws; David's sons show the contradictions of the king, threatening his power and wounding his heart.

6

Father

DAVID HAS been a son: to Jesse, to Saul, and in some manner to Samuel. He has been a brother. He has been a husband. From this moment on in his life, however, the drama of his days is primarily bound up with being a father.

Lord Randolph Churchill, father of Winston Churchill, upon being asked whose descendant he was, prophetically replied, "I am not a descendant; I am an ancestor." It is indeed as an ancestor that David most matters most to the Jewish people because he is considered the forerunner of the Messiah. Still, David's predecessors provide important clues to his character. At this crucial moment when his personal life determines the future course of kingship, echoes of his forerunner Judah are suddenly evoked by a terrible, tragic incident in the life of David's family.

Long before the story of David, back in Genesis, chapter 38, Judah's firstborn son marries Tamar; then he does something "displeasing" to God and dies. In accordance with common practice, Judah marries her to his second son, Onan, who practices coitus interruptus, spilling his seed on the ground and thereby violating the obligation to provide offspring for his deceased brother. Onan dies as well. Judah, although obligated by biblical law to marry his third son to Tamar, evades the responsibility. He fears that the fault lies with her and he will lose yet another son. Tamar, consigned now to unmarriageable widowhood, disguises herself as a prostitute, sleeps with Judah, conceives with him, and then reveals herself. In this crucial moment Judah proves himself capable of nobility. He admits that she is more righteous than he. The child born of this odd union becomes David's ancestor—he is officially in the line of Judah.

That tale is dropped in the middle of the Joseph story back in Genesis, which itself provides many parallels to David. Joseph has dreams that estrange him from his brothers, who seek first to kill him and end up selling him into slavery. The saga of Joseph, in which brothers are entangled in jealousy and repentance, hatreds and near-fratricide, forms the background of the events unfolding in David's house. Many modern scholars believe that the book of Genesis was shaped to support the Davidic claims to kingship. The stories of the patriarchs and their families certainly enrich our understanding of David's life and struggle. Genesis is a saga of siblings and of parents and children. Joseph, the cast-off brother, succeeds, as does David, the neglected youngest. Judah, the brother who will offer to sacrifice himself for Joseph, will be David's ancestor. And we are about to hear the echoes of the first Tamar, the ancestor of David with whom Judah has a child, in the story of the second, David's daughter.

There are different accounts of the number of David's children. Altogether he has, according to the most reliable source, nineteen sons and one daughter who are named, in addition to numerous unnamed sons and daughters. His firstborn is Amnon. His third-born, from a wife named Ma'acah, daughter of Talmai, king of Geshur, was Absalom. We know little of Ma'acah other than that she had the knack for breeding exquisite children.

Absalom has a beautiful sister named Tamar. Amnon, half-brother to Absalom and Tamar, becomes infatuated with her. It appears that there was no absolute prohibition on sleeping with one's half-sister; the reason the text offers for Amnon's thwarted desire is not consanguinity but that Tamar is a virgin. Her virginity means that he cannot sleep with her unless he intends to marry her. Amnon's impulses are more carnal than romantic.

Amnon's friend (and cousin) Jonadab helps formulate a plan for Amnon to be alone with the object of his obsession. Jonadab advises Amnon to play sick and ask for Tamar to bring him food. Jonadab suggests that Amnon ask his half-brother, Absalom, to send Tamar to him. Amnon does not speak with Absalom, however; instead, he asks his father, David, to send Tamar. Perhaps Amnon knew that David would be more easily manipulated than Absalom, less suspicious, more like the biblical Jacob, who blithely sent his son Joseph to his brothers, who then plotted to kill him. An inattentive father is easily coaxed into collusion. Whatever Amnon's reasoning, David complies, and thereby becomes a facilitator of rape.

Tamar brings Amnon food, but instead of eating, he sends everyone away except for Tamar. He asks her to bring the food into the inner chamber, and when she enters, he grabs her. "Come lie with me, my sister" (2, 13:12).

This moment will have endless unfolding consequences for David, for Israel, and for Jewish history.

Like the spirited ancestor for whom she may well have been named, Tamar resists: "Don't, my brother, don't abuse me, for it should not be done thus in Israel, don't do this scurrilous thing. And I, where would I carry my shame? And you, you would be like one of the scurrilous fellows in Israel. And so, speak to the king, for he will not withhold me from you" (2, 13:12–13). In her brief speech, Tamar appeals to Amnon's affection for her, his regard for his own reputation and the prospect of getting what he wants legitimately—insisting that David would permit them to marry. (Whether David would have granted the request is beside the point; at the moment it is a stratagem.) But Amnon's lust overrides any argument. Disregarding her words, he rapes her.

When he is done, "And Amnon hated her with a very great hatred, for greater was the hatred with which he hated her than the love with which he had loved her" (2, 13:15). Thousands of years later readers still feel the cruelty of this event that will alter Israelite history. And even at this remove we feel the force of psychological realism: Amnon has been driven by wild, brutal lust and now is seized by hatred, blaming Tamar for the villainy he himself has perpetrated. He sends her away and Tamar protests. Now she is unable to marry and is in an even worse position than the woman who marries her rapist. According to Jewish law, the rapist is not permitted to send his victim away if she elects to remain with him. So dire is her prospective status that Tamar asks to stay. But Amnon rejects her, compounding his original evil: "And he called his lad, his attendant, and said, 'Send this creature, pray, away from me, and bolt the door behind her!'" (2, 13:17). The Hebrew is even more cutting: send "zot," meaning "this," away from me. Absalom tries to comfort Tamar, and of her subsequent fate we know only the following: "And Tamar stayed, desolate, in the house of Absalom her brother" (2, 13:21).

What follows are these two portentous verses: "And King David had heard all these things, and he was greatly incensed. And Absalom did not speak with Amnon either evil or good, for Absalom hated Amnon for having abused Tamar his sister" (2, 13:21–22).

David is angry but does nothing. In the version of the book of Samuel discovered at the desert caves Qumran dating from the first century CE, and the Septuagint, the early Greek translation of the bible completed around the third century BCE, there is an additional phrase not found in biblical text: "But he did not trouble Amnon, for he loved him, since he was his first-born." Some scholars believe this to be original, but it seems that translator and commentator Robert Alter is correct when he says it is more likely an explanatory gloss: It tells us why David did nothing. There may be other reasons for David's inaction. Perhaps he is so keenly aware of his own infidelity that guilt undermines his sense of moral or parental authority. Or his anger may be less over the injustice than over the disturbance in his household, and, like a modern public figure who wants any scandal swiftly swept under the carpet, he wishes the entire incident to fade as quickly as possible.

This added phrase, "for he loved him," is the only instance in which David is said explicitly to love someone. And it may in fact have been added centuries after the original writing. Shadings of David's character are here highlighted with inadvertent poignancy: The one unambiguous mention of love is found in early translations of the book of Samuel but not in the text as we currently have it. David, always functioning on the edges of love, both basking in it and suffering its consequences, is said to love only in a later rendition of the text. So the question of whether David could love is raised here not only through the story but through the very history of textual transmission, how the story was told and passed along. If it was added later, the author might be looking to explicitly declare this baffling man capable of love.

Earlier, God has instructed David through Nathan in the ways of a parent. In 1 Samuel 7:14, God says that David's offspring will err, and God will chastise them but never withdraw divine love. In other words, God's love, as modeled for David, includes discipline as well as embrace. David himself now proves incapable of the parental task of loving discipline.

We do not know why David was silent after his daughter's

rape. There is no doubt, however, about his third son's motivation; Absalom's silence is clearly calculated. Absalom is biding his time. Two years after his brother's crime, Absalom persuades his father to have Amnon accompany him to the sheep shearing. Once again, David's motivations are murky. David refuses when Absalom asks him to come along. But after some persuasion, David gives permission for Absalom to bring Amnon. Does he believe that Absalom has forgiven his brother? Is David enabling others—as he did when he sent Tamar to Amnon in the first place—while keeping himself at a distance?

David's division of heart is a leitmotif of his personality. He is incensed at Amnon, yet it has been years since the offense. Whether his seeming obliviousness to the possibility of revenge is due to inattention or something more sinister—the desire to see Amnon punished but the inability to do so himself—one motivation alone may not suffice to explain David's reaction. In view of his later mourning, it appears unlikely that he consciously anticipates the result of his actions. But recall that back in Genesis, Jacob too "kept in mind" that the brothers hated Joseph yet sent Joseph off to report on his brothers (Gen. 37:11 ff.), leading to Joseph's enslavement. The Bible often presents the converse to the Oedipus complex: In place of the desire of children to destroy their parents, the Bible unearths the buried drive of parents to destroy their children. It has been called the Isaac complex, because of the twenty-second chapter of Genesis, when Abraham takes Isaac up to the mountain to sacrifice him to God.

The story of Abraham has generated endless commentary. Taken as a psychodynamic portrait of parents and children, however, that example, alongside Saul's attempts on the lives of both Jonathan and David and Jephtah's sacrifice of his daughter (Jud. 11), teaches that the Tanach is acutely aware of the way in which parents at times both love their children and wreck them. David may indeed love Amnon and still send him off with Absalom with the intent, perhaps unconscious, of having Absalom inflict punishment he could not bear to exact himself. Through both action and inaction David causes the collapse of his home and imperils his kingdom. The French philosopher Marquis de Mirabeau was called the "friend of man." At the end of his life his son bitterly remarked, "The 'friend of man' was friend to neither wife nor child." Surely David's wives and children could have offered the same lament.

Successful in getting his father to agree to Amnon's accompanying him to the annual sheep shearing, Absalom sets his plan in motion. He commands his servants that once Amnon is drunk, they should kill him.

Amnon is slain in the field, "basadeh," the same word used when Cain slays his brother Abel. The false rumor reaches David that Absalom has killed all the rest of David's sons. David tears his garment and lies on the ground. He is then told by Jonadab (who first facilitated the encounter between Amnon and Tamar) that only Amnon has been killed. It is almost a distorted photographic reversal of the story of Jacob: All the brothers reported to Jacob that Joseph had been killed when indeed he was alive; David is told all his sons are dead but in fact "only" one of them was killed.

The mourning we witness is in stark contrast to the David who rose as soon as the baby died whom he had sired with Bathsheba. The reported wholesale slaughter of his sons has left him bereft. His future is destroyed by the hand, he believes, of his own child. Even after he discovers that Amnon alone has died, David remains, in the wake of this gruesome pageant of rape, incest, and fratricide, with a house divided against itself. When his other sons return, they weep alongside the king and all his servants.

There is a powerful and suggestive ambiguity in the weeping. The following verse reads, "And Absalom had fled, and he went to Talmai son of Amihur king of Geshur. And David mourned for his son all the while" (2, 13:37). Classical commentators and most moderns assume that by the phrase "his son" Amnon is intended, but several point to the possibility that it is Absalom whom David mourns. In Genesis, when Jacob steals the birthright from his twin brother, Esau, his mother, Rebecca, who has engineered the deception, tells Jacob to run away, lest she lose both children in one day (Gen. 27:45). Without parsing David's ragged emotions at such a time, surely the pain of one son's death and another's murderous action and flight suffice to assume that he was mournful, angry, and bewildered over the disastrous turn of events.

Did David reflect on the parallels between his own conduct and that of his children? He took Bathsheba, no matter the cost, in the manner of Amnon with Tamar. That coupling also resulted in a murder—the orchestrated killing of Bathsheba's husband Uriah. Through multiple mirrors David is reflected in his children. Amnon's sexual voracity is no less part of David's character than are Tamar's eloquence or Absalom's cunning. His children display all the contradictory qualities of their father, and as so often happens in David's life, the result is calamitous. Surely at this moment he recalls the prophecy of Nathan in the aftermath of Uriah's murder: "I am about to raise up evil against you from your own house" (2, 12:11).

Absalom stays away for three years. During that time we may imagine that he both nurses a grudge against the father who does not summon him back and solidifies his justification for what he has done.

The idea that David may in fact be mourning Absalom and Amnon simultaneously is supported by what follows: "And Joab the son of Zeruiah knew that the king's mind was on Absalom" (2, 14:1). The word "on" in Hebrew is "al," which could mean on or against. Once more, the ambiguity of the text suggests David's divided heart. Absalom is his son and his son's slayer. David could be angry or yearning, but most likely both.

Joab decides that it is important for Absalom to return. The decision proves ruinous and Joab's motives uncertain. Perhaps he thinks it will restore David's equilibrium and be good for his rule. Perhaps he has some inkling that Absalom might rebel and wishes to be in good graces with him should the rebellion succeed, though that seems less likely. Either way, we are reminded that Joab's cunning often exceeds his wisdom. Absalom's return enables him to foment rebellion.

How to change the king's mind about allowing Absalom to reenter the kingdom? Joab recruits a "wise woman" of Tekoa and coaches her on what to say to David. (Part of the encounter is dialogue, so she has general guidelines but also improvises.) He advises her to refrain from oil—that is, ancient cosmetics—and to come before the king as one in mourning.

Kings are expected to listen to the grievances of the common people. This remained true long after David: The Roman emperor Hadrian (who ruled 117–38 CE) was traveling on an Italian country road when a peasant woman approached, waving a petition and saying, "Emperor, hear my petition!" When he replied that he did not have time, she responded, "Then stop being emperor!"

David does not wish to stop being king. So he responds when the woman of Tekoa flings herself on the ground and begs for help. She tells him that she is a widow with two sons. They argued in the field (exactly, in another echo, as did Cain and Abel) and one killed the other. Now the people of her town demand the death of her other son, which will "quench my last remaining ember, leaving my husband no name or remnant on the face of the earth" (2, 14:7). David tells her that he will personally issue a decree to save her son. She further asks that no guilt attach to her house and no one be permitted to avenge the blood of her son by killing her remaining living son. To all of this David quickly agrees.

She then switches subjects, asking David why he has done

a similar thing to God's people in not bringing back his own banished son. "For we surely will die, like water spilled to the ground, which cannot be gathered again" (2, 14:14).

Having broached the question of Absalom, at the end of her speech the woman returns to the subject of her son, perhaps fearing that she has overstepped. When she concludes, fluttering and praising David, he asks, "Is the hand of Joab with you in all this?" She admits that Joab was involved. Rather than becoming incensed, David summons him and instructs him to bring Absalom back.

Genesis is a book of brothers: Cain and Abel, Isaac and Ishmael, Jacob and Esau, Joseph and his brothers. The theme continues in Samuel: David knows two pairs of brothers, one of whom dies: his first son with Bathsheba, brother to Solomon, and now Amnon and Absalom. Later the pattern will recur with two sons of David who will vie for kingship: Adonijah and again the surviving Solomon. So the plea is calculated to speak not only to the current situation but to something both in biblical history and in David's life.

Surely the touchstone in David's own life explains in part why the petition succeeds. Additionally, the woman's distress (feigned though it may be) moves David and disposes him to mercy. More immediately it is a double reminder of mortality that touches the king's heart. What she says about Amnon, that death is final, must stir David's memories of his first child with Bathsheba ("I will go to him but he will not return to me"), as well as of Jonathan, and perhaps even of Saul. David is a warrior and has seen plenty of death. But in his personal life, he resembles many of us who keep death at a distance, acknowledging its reality but refusing to face its harsh irrevocability. The wise woman of Tekoa's words revive the sting. What has now happened to two of his children, Bathsheba's first child and Amnon, will happen to Absalom; it will happen to David too. If he wishes to avert death before death—that is, to forestall the distance and silence that death creates while they are both alive—he must let his son return. In this, perhaps, is the woman's insight. By insinuation, metaphor, and simple directness, she restores the pain of death to a man who has seen much of it and run from his own culpability. She may well have been coached in this by Joab, who, although a brutal man himself, surely knows well David's reactions to losing soldiers and sons from their time on the battlefield together.

But self-awareness and fresh perspectives have their limitations. Insights stretch us to the limit of our capacities but not beyond. David will bring Absalom back, but he will do it reluctantly. He still cannot bear to be in his presence. "And the king said, 'Let him turn round to his house, and my face he shall not see.' And Absalom turned round to his house, and the king's face he did not see" (2, 14:24).

When Samuel first came to anoint David, many years before, God warned Samuel that outward appearances did not determine the worthiness of a man for kingship, for God sees into the heart (1, 16:7). David's older brother Eliab may be handsome, God is saying, but David has the soul of a king. Now we are told: "And there was no man so highly praised for beauty as Absalom in all Israel—from the sole of his foot to the crown of his head, there was no blemish in him" (2, 14:25). Beauty in the Bible is almost a guarantee of trouble. Even when we are told more moderately about David, early on, that he is "goodly to look on" it portends troubling consequences. Absalom is described as without blemish. One cannot help but be reminded that according to biblical law, only an animal without blemish is appropriate for sacrifice, foreshadowing Absalom's fate.

Despite the Bible's general reluctance to offer specific, physical descriptions, the weight and luxuriance of Absalom's hair is scrupulously described. This is a reminder not only of the bizarre way in which he will die, with his hair (the text says "head") entangled in a tree, but of Samson, another biblical figure whose strength was sapped by a haircut. Both Absalom and Samson had charisma; each had an adolescent streak; both burned fields; both died by their locks. We know that hair is somehow tied to downfall and/or deception, not only in Samson's case, where Delilah betrays him by wheedling and shearing (Jud. 16), but in the case of Jacob, who deceives his blind father by pasting sheepskins on his arms, since Esau is hairy and Jacob smooth (Gen. 27).

The final bit of introduction tells us that Absalom had three sons and a beautiful daughter named Tamar. The naming of his daughter after his defiled sister is a reminder of Absalom's original wound, the rape of Tamar by Amnon, the incident that precipitated the breach with his father. The medieval commentator Abravanel at this point makes the perceptive comment that the Bible is telling us of David's grandchildren to emphasize that even their existence did not persuade David to reconcile with Absalom.

For two years Absalom lives in Jerusalem and David will not see him. Desperado fashion, Absalom has his servants set fire to Joab's barley field (these are remarkably loyal servants—they also killed Amnon on Absalom's behalf). Here is an example of the Tanach's subtle semantic hints, since the Hebrew words for barley and hair are related, barley being the "bearded" grain. When Joab upbraids Absalom for burning his field, the prodigal responds that if the king will not see him, he ought never to have come home. If he is guilty, let the king decree death upon him; otherwise, it is time to end the estrangement. Absalom never offers a justification for burning Joab's fields. Implicit is that any means are justified for Absalom in pursuit of his ends.

A vain and self-involved child meets an ineffective parent. David is unable to provide the sort of consistent, steady, boundaried, but deep love that is a parent's job. With Amnon he was vastly overindulgent. With Tamar he was seemingly absent. With

Absalom he is repeatedly harsh and remote. Before we witnessed a David who, in intimate relationships, swung from passionate involvement to bewildering distance. He was intensely enmeshed with Bathsheba in a wildly uneven tale of lust and murder; with his first wife, Michal, he insisted upon her returning to him and then, after a fairly trivial dispute, remained far from her all of her remaining days. The pattern holds here as well. Emotionally erratic, David will tolerate Absalom living in his sphere of influence (perhaps he suspects rebellious tendencies?), but he will not come close. Being a leader is not the same as being a parent. Nonetheless, David still knows how to listen: When Joab petitions him, he agrees to see Absalom. In the encounter David, who has made his mark as a commander, falls back on this primary role instead of being a father. The private David is increasingly swallowed by the public David. The Bible informs us of David's distance in a quiet but devastating way when Absalom is brought before him.

"And he called to Absalom and he came to the king and bowed down to him, his face before the king, and the king kissed Absalom" (2, 14:33). Notice that Absalom is not kissed by his father or by David; he is kissed by "the king." In a single verse, David is referred to as "the king" three times. After a many-staged reconciliation, a father's bearing in a moment of presumed reconciliation has reverberations in the psyche of any child. Reinforcing this is the observation of the medieval commentator Ralbag (Gersonides) that in the Hebrew the king kissed "L'Abshalom" not "et Abshalom"—the former implying a more distant kiss, on the hand or shoulder.

Given what we will see later in David's mourning for Absalom, this scene suggests not a lack of love but something worse —a refusal to love. There is an almost monstrous quality in his self-restraint with his own child. It is not anger, which implies intimacy, but the cold, cloaked dissociation of a man whose heart is unavailable to himself, and therefore to his child. Given the long history among ruling clans of family usurpations, David would have done well to understand what Louis XIV expressed centuries later, that if he must fight, it should be with his enemies and not with his children.

Absalom, who has been introduced with clear overtones of narcissism touching on his beauty and his hair, is doubtless deeply wounded by the chilly reception. Perhaps the seeds of rivalry had been sown before, but now he decides to treat his father not as a father but as an obstacle to the throne he covets. Absalom nurtures his rebellion slowly and methodically.

What do we know of his character up until now? Absalom was outraged by the violation of his sister. His response was calculating, patient, and brutal. He waited two years to exact his revenge, and it was done not by his own hand but by his servants. Then, by the agency of Joab he was restored to Jerusalem, though not to his father's presence. Again, his response was deliberate and destructive. He had his servants set fire to Joab's field, without any indication that he had tried less savage ways to engage the warrior's attention.

He is beautiful, and we will see his charm and cleverness, but there is surely reason to doubt his judgment and fitness to rule.

The tenor of Absalom's character is set by this sentence, which chronicles his activity right after he has been forced to leave David: "And it happened thereafter that Absalom made himself a chariot with horses and fifty men running before him" (2, 15:1). Absalom's response to dismissal is grandiosity. He will gradually seek to usurp his father's place. When people come to plead a case before David, Absalom will intercept them and tell them that their cause is just, but that "you have no one to listen to you from the king" (2, 15:3).

This response is both politically astute and personally resonant. As Absalom was not listened to by his father, he plays on the people's sense of being ignored. He tells Israel that if he were judge in the land, he would listen and rule in their favor. Insisting to people that one would rule in their favor is, of course, the tactic of the demagogue; no one can know without hearing a suit what the result should be. But Absalom assures the questioner because currying approval is more important than justice. There is always dissatisfaction with government and disgruntled plaintiffs at law. A beautiful man, son of the king, tells petitioners they are getting a bad deal. "And Absalom stole the hearts of the men of Israel" (2, 15:6).

For four years (the Masoretic text has forty, but four is almost certainly intended) Absalom curries favor with the people. He has carefully built his base, and all is prepared. He asks David leave to go to Hebron to fulfill an earlier vow to offer a sacrifice. Permission being granted (has David no idea what his son is plotting?), Absalom takes with him two hundred men and Ahitophel, David's own adviser. There, in Hebron, where David had begun his kingship, Absalom launches his rebellion.

Absalom's rebellion engulfs the nation in war. Why has he been able to muster such opposition to David?

The story provides its own justifications. Sentiment supporting Saul and his house remains, and David is still suspected of having played a part in its downfall. David's very public sin with Bathsheba and Uriah remains notorious. Also, David has been frequently involved in war, the reason given in Chronicles for his not having been permitted to build the Temple. Jewish authorities from the Talmud on to medievals like Nahmanides believe that David engaged in *milchamot reshut*—that is, voluntary wars, rather than battles of self-defense or legitimate boundary wars. Since wars involve conscription, death, taxes, and many sacrifices from noncombatants as well, the people are exhausted.

Add to the mix the inevitable disillusionments with any administration, Absalom's charisma, and opportunities for those who have not risen in David's crew to do so with a new regime. There may well have been other, local grievances lost to us.

Finally, there is David's own inability to see the looming threat. David's blindness is confounding. He is hardly a stranger to schemes and is surrounded by veteran fighters. Does no one around him warn him of Absalom's systematic erosion of his authority?

As a youth, David won God's favor and went on to use it to commit adultery and murder. Then he saw his own children rape and kill one another. His anger at Absalom may well have an element of self-loathing, or his obliviousness to Absalom's scheme may mask a covert impulse to self-destruction. The rabbinic Midrash picks up this theme in a way that anticipates Søren Kierkegaard's powerful opening story in "Fear and Trembling," an extended meditation on the binding of Isaac (Gen. 22). Kierkegaard imagines that Abraham angrily proclaims to Isaac that it is Abraham's choice to kill Isaac, that he has always hated him. When the patriarch's hand is stayed by an angel, the pretense collapses. Abraham weeps and confesses to Isaac, "I thought it better you should hate me than hate God." Similarly in the Talmud, the Rabbis imagine a scenario in which David tells his adviser Hushai that he plans to give the people an excuse to blame him instead of God for Absalom's uprising: He will start worshiping idols, and Israel will assume it was his faithlessness that caused the upheaval (San. 107a).

A different attempt to explain David's blindness to brewing insurrection involves his susceptibility to deception. Remember that David was deceived by Nathan's parable before being told that it is in fact about him and Bathsheba. He was deceived by the woman of Tekoa, whom Joab sent to reconcile the king to Absalom. He was deceived by permitting Tamar to go to her brother and rapist Amnon, and by permitting Amnon to go to sheep shearing with Absalom. Given that David, cunning himself, seems always to underestimate the cunning of others, perhaps he simply does not credit Absalom's craftiness. Sometimes the deceiver is oblivious of the power of others to deceive.

Then of course there is the naïveté that so often befogs parents. Since David remained far from Absalom emotionally, he could not see his son in his fullness: The same man whose motives he misread, whose forgiveness he denied, is now the man whose intentions he ignores. When David was young, the Israelites poured onto the streets proclaiming that Saul had killed thousands and David tens of thousands. Now the pattern is repeating itself: David is king, but Absalom is gradually winning the people's hearts. Whereas the shift in popular acclaim drove Saul into paranoia, David does not even appear cognizant of it. One king suffered from too much noticing, the other from too little.

However, sweet oblivion cannot last. An informant comes to David and apprises him of Absalom's revolt. Alert and alarmed, David prepares an escape, throwing his team into a sudden frenzy of activity.

The king flees with his household and servants, including a band of those, not Israelites by birth, who owe David personal loyalty: Cherethites and Pelethites, his guard, and Githites, who have remained with him since his days fighting in Philistine territories. David has always been scrupulously fair with his men, and now he gives them the opportunity to remain and join with Absalom. Ittai the Gittite answers nobly: "As the Lord lives, and as my lord the king lives, whatever place that my lord the king may be, whether for death or for life, there your servant will be" (2, 15:21). This recalls the speech of another foreigner, David's ancestor Ruth, who joined another wandering Judean, Naomi (Ruth 1:16–17). Such echoes remind the reader of the rewards of fidelity to God's chosen ones.

So David, king of Israel, flees from his capital, flees from his son, and leaves "ten concubines" to watch over his house. As philosopher Martin Buber points out, David's life is determined by two stories of flight: first from Saul and then from Absalom. In a deep sense, first from his father and then from his son.

The dual images of David—the blessed man, marching to Jerusalem with the recovered ark, whirling and dancing before God, now become the hunted leader, frightened and fleeing with a ragtag band composed mostly of non-Israelites—form a searing diptych of downfall. "And David was going up the Slope of Olives, going up weeping, his head uncovered and he walking barefoot, and all the people who were with him, everyone with his head uncovered, went on up weeping the while" (2, 15:30).

This indelible scene of the king weeping as he walks is both a presage of the later exile of Israel in subsequent generations and a profile of the penitent. David's scalding line about Saul and Jonathan in his elegy—How the mighty have fallen!—might well be the caption on the image of his march to save himself from his own son. Yet now, crying and humbled, he renews his communication with God. His fortunes have fallen to their lowest point as he reaches out to God while praying for his former adviser Ahitophel's counsel to be frustrated, a prayer that will indeed be granted.

At this desolate moment there is a reminder of David's spiritual sensitivities. The Levites carry the ark with him as he flees, and he instructs them to go back and return the ark to Jerusalem, where it belongs: God, he says, will return him to Jerusalem if he is meant to be there, but in any event, the ark should remain in its rightful place.

This is the sort of double shaded declaration that makes David so extraordinary. For it is, without doubt, a statement of his faith. David, who brought the ark to Jerusalem, believes that it belongs in its eternal home. That is part of the mission of his kingship, the rock on which it rests. In his darkness his compass of trust in God still proves true. At the same time, however, we must wonder: The Levites who carried the ark are clearly loyal to him. If he returns them to Jerusalem, where Absalom will shortly take over the city and his house, will they not serve as an intelligence network for David? Could his professed piety be both sincere and calculating? Only the reader who has not followed David's exploits until now would dismiss the possibility. He may be a man without a kingdom or a home, but he is never a man without a resource.

The combination of piety and practicality arises almost immediately upon his abandoning Jerusalem. Knowing that Ahitophel, once his own counselor, has begun to advise Absalom, David prays to God that Ahitophel's sage instructions be thwarted. At that moment, on the summit of the Mount of Olives, David looks up and sees Hushai the Archite coming toward him. Hushai's tunic is torn, and he has earth on his head, both signs of mourning—in other words, signs that he is loyal to David.

Hushai plans to flee with David, but the king has a better idea: Go back to Jerusalem, pretend loyalty to Absalom, and confound Ahitophel's counsel. Discover what Absalom intends and inform the priests (remember, David has returned the ark to Jerusalem), who will report back to me. Hushai, identified as "David's friend," returns to Jerusalem just as Absalom enters the city.

Saul's house is not done haunting David. David is pursued by Shimei ben Gera, a Benjaminite who curses at the fleeing king, hurling stones at David and his retinue. Since Shimei seems at the moment to be alone, this is not a calculated attack but an explosion of rage. He is furious: "Get out, get out, you man of blood, you worthless fellow! The Lord has brought back to you all the blood of the house of Saul, in whose place you became king . . . " (2, 16:7–8). In the Anchor Bible series, scholar P. Kyle McCarter gives Shimei's curse a plausible and more colorful translation: "You bloodstained fiend of hell!"

The rumors of David's involvement in the death of those who were "Saul's house"—his commander Abner, his son Ish-Bosheth, perhaps Saul and Jonathan themselves—clearly pursue David and provide one of the grounds for grievance against him. What Shimei expresses is unlikely to be particular to one man (as evidenced by a thousand other northerners in a later reconciliation scene with David). The care with which the story explains that David is innocent of their blood reinforces the plausibility, if not the accuracy, of the accusation. Surely those who were partisans of Saul find it hard to credit that the collapse of his line and the death of his sons and military chief have nothing whatsoever to do with his son-in-law and nemesis.

We learn of David's reaction to Shimei's vilification from his statement to one of his more volatile soldiers. Joab is David's commander, and we have seen his machinations and violent disposition. Joab's brother, Abishai, is cut from the same cloth. It was actually Abishai who accompanied David when he crept up alongside Saul, and Abishai who proposed to kill the king as he slept (1, 26). At that time David curbed Abishai's regicidal impulse. Abishai's military prowess, similar to that of his brother Joab, has proved and will continue to prove important to David. Once again, however, Abishai's first impulse is the sword, and he proposes to cross over to where Shimei ben Gera is cursing and "take off his head" (1, 16:9).

David retains the artful equanimity that won him the kingship, and again restrains Abishai from murder. He says, in effect, to Abishai: Look, my own son is seeking to kill me, so should we be surprised that this Benjaminite (that is, someone from Saul's home territory) feels the same? "Perhaps the Lord will see my affliction and the Lord may requite me good for his cursing this day" (2, 16:12). David simultaneously trusts God's ultimate judgment and understands Shimei's resentment. He will remember the insubordinate cursing, but he will not, right now, seek to punish it. An effective king must exhibit self-restraint and take the long view.

David has been stripped of self-righteousness. From the moment that Nathan said to him, "You are the man," he has understood that consequences will follow his own sins. Lacking the unreflective assurance of a less thoughtful man, he appreciates that Shimei and others have legitimate grievances. Trusting God's estimation of his own character and intentions, he does not assume that all who oppose him must be misguided or evil. This is of a piece with David's capacity to listen. There is an empathetic quality to his character because of the breadth of his internal experience which permits him to mirror those who touch his life: He understood Saul's melancholy when little more than a child, appreciated the Philistine king's predicament well enough to ingratiate himself, absorbed Nathan's rebuke, heard sympathetically the Tekoa woman's story and now Shimei's disdain.

As Shimei continues to hurl insults and stones, David marches on with his troops. Angry echoes accompany each footstep. There is something majestic about the king who will not pursue his tormentor. What distinguishes David from those around him is that there is no single note that captures his protean personality. In both the classical and the scholarly literature, the disagreement about his essential nature is striking, ranging from saintliness to ruthlessness. In his refusal to strike at Shimei and in not further riling up the North, we see political pragmatism; in his certainty that he must submit to God's will, a deep faith; and in understanding that he has not been assured the loyalty of Saul's tribe, political sagacity. Through it all, however, Abishai marches beside him, because David is sufficiently powerful and charismatic to retain the loyalty of even this cutthroat warrior. And as Abishai no doubt suspects, David will not forget what Shimei has done this day.

Psalm 3 is traditionally ascribed to David as he flees from his son.

> A psalm of David. When he fled from his son Absalom.
>
> ¹ Lord, how many are my foes!
> How many rise up against me!
> ² Many are saying of me,

"God will not deliver him."
3 But you, Lord, are a shield around me,
my glory, the One who lifts my head high.
4 I call out to the Lord,
and he answers me from his holy mountain.
5 I lie down and sleep;
I wake again, because the Lord sustains me.
6 I will not fear though tens of thousands
assail me on every side.
7 Arise, Lord!
Deliver me, my God!
Strike all my enemies on the jaw;
break the teeth of the wicked.
8 From the Lord comes deliverance.
May your blessing be on your people.

This psalm conveys both the terror and the faith of David as he runs from his own son. One chapter earlier, Psalm 2 describes the battle of all the nations, an apocalyptic war. Yet the Talmud notes that the second psalm does not contain a verse expressing pain the way the third psalm does. The Rabbis conclude, "Harsher is the effect of bad upbringing of children in a man's house than even the war of Gog and Magog [that is, the battle of the apocalypse]" (Berachot 7b). For king or commoner, the pain in families dwarfs even the final, eschatological battle.

David's salvation, for which he both prayed and plotted, is indeed found in his friend Hushai, surreptitiously sent by David to betray the rebellion. Hushai's approach to Absalom is clever and laced with double meanings. "Long live the king, long live the king!" (2, 16:17), begins Hushai. Of course, he does not pronounce Absalom's name, and his repetition of the phrase suggests there are, at present, two kings. Neither meaning is explicit. When Absalom asks him why he is not serving his friend David, Hushai answers, "Whom the Lord has chosen, and this people and every man of Israel—his I will be and with him I will stay . . . " (16:18). Each word from Hushai's mouth is open to more than one interpretation. Absalom, though he has shown himself charming, patient, and savagely effective, is missing what self-aggrandizing people often lack—an ear for irony.

Upon advice from David's former confidant Ahitophel, Absalom asserts his primacy by sleeping with his father's concubines "before the eyes of all Israel" (2, 16:22). Nathan's curses from the Bathsheba episode are coming to pass: "He shall lie with your wives in the sight of the sun" (2, 12:11). Some commentators speculate that Absalom selects the very roof where David spotted Bathsheba and thereby set the disaster in motion, to show an irreconcilable divide between himself and his father. Everyone in Israel must choose. As Absalom has taken Jerusalem and demonstrated his potency in every significant sense, his expectation is that he will be chosen.

The decisive moment of the rebellion has arrived. Absalom cannot simply stay in Jerusalem; he must decide how to vanquish his father. Ahitophel gives him sound advice, asking Absalom for twelve thousand troops to pursue David now that he is bedraggled. Ahitophel himself will dispatch "the king" (significant that he still so refers to David), and Absalom will reign. The quick strike, Ahitophel insists, will prove a triumphant strategy.

Absalom approves of the advice, and so do the elders. But he wishes to hear what Hushai has to say as well. A CIA report declassified in 1994 evaluates "The Tale of Hushai the Archite." As the report states, in examining the tale of spy and counterspy, "Hushai lost no time in exploiting the distrust, jealousy, fear and guilt complexes inherent in the situation."

Asked to offer advice, Hushai tells Absalom: "The counsel that Ahitophel has given is not good this time" (2, 17:7). He reminds Absalom that David is a seasoned guerrilla fighter. He is not one to be easily taken by surprise and will probably be waiting to pounce on the first troops to show up. Should David win an initial battle, the rumor that the fight is going badly will be injurious to Absalom's cause. Better, says Hushai, to gather together all Israel. Hushai's use of that term signals that there is countrywide support for the revolt, north as well as south.

Hushai may be appealing not only to Absalom's fear of his father's vaunted prowess but to his vanity that he can gather all of Israel to his side. Believing himself to be the favored one, Absalom decides that he has little to lose. Ahitophel, of course, has estimated probabilities far better. But Absalom opts to follow Hushai's advice: "And the Lord had ordained to overturn Ahitophel's good counsel in order for the Lord to bring evil on Absalom" (2, 17:14). Here is the familiar double causation: Both Hushai's skill and God's decree seem to play a part in Absalom's fateful mistake.

Delay permits David to escape a rout. When the informants run and tell David what has happened, he quickly makes his way with his troops across the Jordan. He cannot not flee north or south, both regions being preserves of Absalom loyalists. To run to the sea would put him in Philistine territory, equally dangerous. So David runs just as Saul had long before, across the Jordan, where he and his troops refresh themselves.

As the fighting approaches its climax, David's former adviser Ahitophel, whose wise words have been disregarded by Absalom, makes a strange choice. He returns to his home, puts his affairs in order, and hangs himself. Perhaps it is an act of honor. He may assume that David will now win and he will suffer for his betrayal. Or even that if Absalom wins, he will no longer retain his position. Either way, the Tanach reports the suicide dispassionately. There is not a word of approval or, as might be expected, condemnation. The end of Ahitophel is rendered with austere dignity.

Meanwhile, Absalom appoints a military chief, Amasa, who appears to be, like Joab, a nephew of David's and according to Chronicles (1, 12:19), an early David supporter. He has now turned to Absalom.

David retains sufficient loyalty to prevail, however. The denouement is bizarre and quick. David divides his troops into thirds and gives them one directive—to "deal gently" with Absalom. David wishes to win and retain his kingship but not to see the death of still another child.

The battle takes place in the forest of Ephraim. In a striking line we are told that "the forest devoured more of the troops than the sword that day" (2, 18:8). The early Aramaic translation, cited by the medieval commentator Rashi, says that this verse refers to wild beasts. Whatever the narrative intent, the forest does, in a strange way, devour Absalom.

Astride his donkey, Absalom catches his head in the tangle of a tree. Although the Talmud, and most readers, assume that it is his hair that gets caught, the text itself says that it is his head, as though it was the offending organ. A man reports to Joab that Absalom is physically suspended between heaven and earth. Joab, insisting that he would have rewarded the man handsomely to finish him off, asks why he left Absalom alive? The answer alerts us that David's plea to spare his son has been widely heard: "Even were I to heft a thousand pieces of silver, I would not reach out my hand against the king's son, for within our hearing the king charged you and Abishai and Ittai, saying, 'Watch for me over the lad Absalom.' Otherwise I would have wrought falsely with my own life, and nothing can be concealed from the king, while you would have stood aloof" (2, 18:12–14). The instruction has gone to all three of David's commanders, and the troops have overheard them as well. The man who witnesses Absalom dangling helplessly justifiably assumes that to kill him would bring him a death sentence from David, in accordance with his long-standing practice of killing those who dispatch his enemies.

But Joab, the soldier-thug, is neither satisfied nor deterred. He hates Absalom for challenging his king, disrespecting his father, and burning Joab's fields. Victory is within easy grasp.

Joab strikes Absalom with three darts (one each, say the Rabbis seeking moral symmetry, for stealing the heart of his father, David, the hearts of Israel, and the heart of the court, since Absalom said, "Would that I were made Judge in the land" 2, 15:4; JT. Sotah 1:7). It is a moment that recalls David's words of comfort to the wise woman of Tekoa about the fate of her sons in the parable: "As the Lord lives," David promised her, "not a single hair of your son's shall fall to the ground" (2, 14:11). Inversely echoing the prophecy, Absalom hangs defenseless, dying as his hair suspends him in midair.

Absalom is dispatched by Joab plus "ten lads," and his body is flung into a pit in the forest and covered with stones.

Joab sounds the horn and "Israel" flees—that is, all those who followed Absalom. We are now told that before his rebellion, Absalom had built a monument, a cairn, because he said, "I have no son to make my name remembered" (2, 18:18). Absalom, the son who rebelled against his father, himself has no child to enshrine his memory or legacy. The anguish of parent-child relations and their absence threads through each nuance of the narrative.

David has, of course, been informed many times of the death of enemies. It has never been like this. Ahimaaz, a liked and trusted Israelite, unaware at first of Absalom's death, wishes to run and tell David of the victory. Joab, knowing that it will be terrible news from a beloved source, discourages him and sends a foreign messenger, a Cushite, in his place. Perhaps Joab fears that David will slay the messenger and therefore does not wish to pick a soldier or valued friend. Ahimaaz decides that he is needed in any case and David sees him running.

David assumes that Ahimaaz must be bringing good news.

"And he bowed down to the king, his face to the ground, and he said, 'Blessed is the Lord your God who has delivered over the men who raised their hand against my lord the king.' And the king said, 'Is it well with the lad Absalom?' And Ahimaaz said, 'I saw a great crowd to send the king's servant Joab, and your servant, and I know not what . . .'"

It seems that Ahimaaz cannot bring himself to speak coherently now that the moment of truth has arrived. David grows impatient:

> And the king said, "Turn aside, stand by!" And he turned aside and took his place. And, look, the Cushite had come and the Cushite said, "Let my lord the king receive the tidings that the Lord has done you justice against all those who rose against you." And the king said to the Cushite, "Is it well with the lad Absalom?" And the Cushite said, "May the enemies of my lord the king be like the lad, and all who have risen against you for evil!" (2, 18:28–32)

Absalom is dead. "And the king was shaken. And he went up to the upper room over the gate and he wept, and thus he said as he went, 'My son, Absalom! My son, my son, Absalom! Would that I had died in your stead! Absalom, my son, my son'" (2, 19:1).

When Saul and Jonathan died, David summoned eloquence. Now, he can barely speak. Some classical commentators, like the nineteenth-century scholar Malbim, write that David is haunted by the thought that Absalom has died for his father's sins, hence David's wish to die in his son's place. But more powerfully, fundamentally, it is a parent's recognition of the wrongness of things. David is no longer that young man who was able to jump back into the world after mourning his first child with Bathsheba, ready to live despite the anguish of loss. Now David is older, weary with loss, the memory of his treatment of Absalom a patchwork of regret.

The Rabbis rush in with interpretations of David's groan of anguish. "Absalom" or "my son" is said by David eight times, each iteration to raise Absalom's soul, in the manner of the mourner's kaddish, to heaven. These and other legends express the sense that David seeks redemption for breeding the resentment that has destroyed Absalom.

This is the moment David has learned to be a father, and it is too late. While his son Solomon will, at David's deathbed, benefit from some of his father's wisdom, the harmony he might have established is clear now in his tidal grief. David has won everything he coveted and lost everything he cared for. This snapshot of agony sums up for generations the price of power, the intersection of family and public life, the way in which we injure ourselves and are then staggered by the pain.

David's anguish and remorse make him an exemplar, in this respect at least, to later generations searching for biblical models. The Puritans turned to David more often than any biblical character except for the New Testament Jesus. For not only is David a military model (as in the sermon by Massachusetts Bay preacher John Richardson: "Thou canst not be too exact in this Art military, make David thy pattern"), but he embodies repentance with Nathan, faith with returning the ark to Jerusalem, and suffering, particularly with Absalom. The very ambiguity of all military conquests—death that for the reflective dampens triumph—is given special poignancy when the commander loses, in his very victory, the son who rebelled. David is a warrior who has suffered, a king who has demonstrated humility, and a father who has both lost and passed on his legacy.

Following the news of Absalom's death, the day of victory becomes for the troops a day of mourning. Stricken to see the king so bereft, the troops themselves are saddened, and as David continues to bewail his son, they steal home with nothing to celebrate despite their sacrifice. Joab, who ensures the victory, who protects David from others, now with a dose of savage honesty, protects David from himself:

> You have today shamed all your servants who have saved
> your life today and the lives of your sons and daughters and
> the lives of your wives and the lives of your concubines, to

love those who hate you and to hate those who love you. For you have said today that you have no commanders or servants. For I know today that were Absalom alive and all of us today dead, then it would have been right in your eyes! And now, rise, go out, and speak to the heart of your servants. For by the Lord I have sworn, if you go not out, that not a man shall spend the night with you, and this will be a greater evil for you than any evil that has befallen you from your youth until now. (2, 19:6–9)

David understands the truth of Joab's words. Once again he proves himself able to listen to the wisdom of others and take action. He cannot muster the strength to speak to the people, so instead David sits in the gate and the people come to him. It is a melancholy scene. David has managed, however, to restore himself enough to ask the priests to speak to the elders of Judah and implore them to renew their fealty to him.

Following the incident with Bathsheba and Uriah, David responded to Nathan's parable of the rich man by proclaiming: "And the poor man's ewe he shall pay back fourfold, in as much as he has done this thing, and because he had no pity" (2, 12:5–6). Rashi comments that David pays fourfold through his children: the first child with Bathsheba who died; the second child Tamar, whom Amnon raped and abandoned; Amnon, who is murdered; and finally Absalom.

7

Caretaker

DAVID RESUMES his responsibilities as king with several lin-
gering effects from battle that must be managed. The closing
chapters of the book of Samuel, before the book of Kings gives
us the succession story, tell of his final active days and efforts to
consolidate the kingdom he will bequeath to his son.

Although he recognizes the justice of restoring Joab to
leadership over the troops, David is not reconciled to the man
who killed his son and then admonished him to disregard his
grief. David turns instead to Amasa, the former leader of Absalom's troops, and asks him to become the head of the army in
place of Joab—a repeat of the maneuver earlier with Abner,
who was the onetime head of Saul's troops. In that instance
Joab, out of both personal pique and concern for "job security,"
killed Abner. It should not surprise us that Amasa will soon
meet the same fate.

As David prepares to recross the Jordan back into his kingdom, Shimei, who had cursed David at the outset of the battle, now returns penitent with a thousand Israelites at his back. The North was traditionally less loyal to David than the South, his natural base in the territory of Judah. Once again, Joab's brother Abishai agitates to kill Shimei. As before, David's equanimity prevails: "'What have I to do with you, sons of Zeruiah, that you should become my adversary today? Should today a man of Israel be put to death? For I surely know that today I am king over Israel.' The king said to Shimei 'You shall not die.' And the king swore to him" (2, 19:23–24). David is king not only of Judah but of the North as well, of all Israel. He must act the king. A nation will not be united with reprisals, so David stays Abishai's hand.

Immediately following David's resumption of rule, arguing breaks out between the northern men of Israel and the southern men of Judah. David's grip remains tenuous, and he does not enter the dialogue. He is drained by Absalom's revolt and death, and returning to Jerusalem does not revivify him. The split between the North and South, the constant, roiling tension that played itself out in Saul versus David early on, has not been healed. North and South will remain united during the reign of Solomon, and then separate until the North is destroyed by the Assyrians some three hundred years later.

In short order there is yet another revolt, this time led by a Benjaminite named Sheba, son of Bichri. Once more a man related to Saul attempts to usurp David's throne. David, fearful now, warns Amasa (his newly appointed chief, alongside a seething Joab) that Sheba may do more harm than Absalom.

The Psalms express what we may take to be David's internal state facing yet another revolt:

> ⁶ I said, "Oh, that I had the wings of a dove!
> I would fly away and be at rest.
> ⁷ I would flee far away

and stay in the desert;
⁸ I would hurry to my place of shelter,
far from the tempest and storm."
⁹ Lord, confuse the wicked, confound their words,
for I see violence and strife in the city.
¹⁰ Day and night they prowl about on its walls;
malice and abuse are within it.
¹¹ Destructive forces are at work in the city;
threats and lies never leave its streets. (Ps. 55)

Knowing that his leadership and life once again are in the balance, David advises immediate pursuit, lest Sheba hide in a fortified, walled town. We remember that this was precisely the strategy Ahitophel recommended to Absalom. Disregarding it cost Absalom the war and his life. David makes no such mistake.

David may have appointed Absalom's old commander Amasa, but with Joab still vital, such an arrangement cannot last. On the way to track down the rebel Sheba, Joab sneaks up and stabs Amasa much as he had his earlier rival Abner. Again the reader is left wondering whether Joab has acted in contravention of David's will or in secret obedience to him. Either way, with yet another rival dispatched, Joab is left to pursue Sheba, who has managed to hide himself in a walled town after all.

Once more in a crisis a woman's wisdom and action save the day and save David, too. An unidentified woman pleads poetically with Joab not to besiege the city: "You seek to put to death a mother city in Israel. Why should you engulf the Lord's heritage?" (2, 20:19). In ancient days, a city siege meant starvation, an inability to get supplies for the diseased and infirm, and the certainty of many deaths. Joab tells her that he does not wish to punish the city; he needs only to eliminate Sheba, who has rebelled against the king.

"And the woman came in her wisdom to all the people, and they cut off the head of Sheba son of Bichri and flung it to

Joab" (2, 20:22). Problem solved. Everyone goes home and Joab returns to Jerusalem.

Women's influence on the course of events in the David story proves crucial and continual. In Saul's moment of desperation he turns to a woman, the Witch of En-Dor. Michal enables David to flee early on and saves his life. Abigail saves David from a crucial political and moral mistake. The woman of Tekoa helps David recognize the responsibility he owes his son. The anonymous woman of the walled city saves the city from siege and the king's representative, Joab, from a bloody and unnecessary battle. Finally, in perhaps the most important moment of historical influence, Bathsheba will persuade David to anoint their son Solomon. Repeatedly women are there to ensure that the men, mostly David, adroitly navigate the alternatives to a successful conclusion.

The prevalence of women signals again the openness of David's spirit. As he listens to his troops, to the prophet, he will also heed the words of the women in his life. Resolute and stubborn in many ways, David also proves accessible and malleable.

The episodes that conclude the book of Samuel all seem as though they are somewhat loose additions, not tied to the narrative as we have known it, and not strictly in its spirit. Yet they too are tightly constructed. As translator Everett Fox writes: "Chapters 21–24 are chiastic (inverted) in structure: David's two last poems (22:1–23:7) are surrounded, first by accounts of his heroes' exploits, and then by two stories of disaster (famine and plague) and relief."

Following the quelling of the rebellion, a famine breaks out which, God tells David, is punishment for a slaughter of the Gibeonites enacted by Saul. We have not been told of any such massacre, but it results in seven of Saul's male descendants being turned over to the Gibeonites, who impale them. David then ensures that Saul and Jonathan are reburied in their home territory.

David has officially eliminated the final remaining challenges to his reign. Saul's line has been an enduring threat to his hegemony. How the Gibeonites are implicated is unclear; but that David has managed, through apparent subterfuge and slaughter, to secure his throne, is made evident.

David launches into an extended poem here which does not entirely fit the story around it. Part of it is an expression of deep faith, "The Lord is my crag and my fortress and my own deliverer" (2, 22:2), and part the kind of poetry one might find in Job or elsewhere in Psalms that seems to have little direct connection to David's life:

> The channels of the sea were exposed
> the world's foundations laid bare,
> by the Lord's roaring,
> the blast of His nostrils.

In this introduction to the final stanzas David is given the famous title "sweet singer of Israel," and surely his reputation as a poet influenced the placement of this ode. Still, it is hard to resist the conclusion of most scholars that an already existing ode was placed here to add a poetic note, concluding as follows:

> Therefore do I praise You, Lord, among nations,
> and to your name do I chant.
> Saving tower to His King,
> standing steadfast by His anointed
> by David and his seed, forever. (2, 22:50–51)

After the poem is a brief tribute to the fighting men who accompanied David throughout his adventures. We are told how David expressed thirst and three warriors broke through Philistine lines to get him water. Rather than drink the water while leaving his soldiers thirsty, and in appreciation for their risk, David pours it out as a libation to God, demonstrating his nobility, his care for his men and his appreciation of their valor.

A remarkable feature of the list of names is that it concludes with "Uriah the Hittite," the very man whose murder David, long before, had engineered so that he might have Bathsheba. Once more the text is pointing to the division inside David: noble and surrounded by those who fought valiantly in his cause, yet among these devoted men is someone David ruthlessly betrayed.

The book of Samuel adds an unedifying tale about a census conducted among the people and a resulting plague. There are multiple taboos against counting people in the ancient world and in Israel, and it was a common practice to substitute a coin or some other token in place of counting heads. Later commentators trace the prohibition to the depredations of the evil eye or the incident of the golden calf, or explain simply that it contradicts the biblical promise that the Israelites will be too numerous to be counted (Gen. 13:16). David is given a choice of punishment by the prophet Gad: seven years of famine, three months of fleeing from enemies, or three days of plague. He chooses plague: "Let us, pray, fall into the Lord's hand, for great is his mercy, and into the hand of man let me not fall" (2, 24:14). This very passage is recited in the daily morning confessional prayers, as a way of acknowledging that God's mercy is greater than that of human beings. David has long experience of the special cruelty of which people are capable. A plague does in fact ravage the people for a time, though there is no mention of losses in David's own house.

David's days as a biblical conquistador have ended. There will be no more battles to win, rebellions to quell, women to woo. His enemies are gone. Israel needs a new king.

8

Death of a King

Davɪᴅ's ɪs a story not only of spirit but of blood and bone and flesh. Spirit animates the tale, but it moves through a somatic world, where ambitious youths run too fast, kings defecate in caves, and arrows pierce enemies. With none of the poetic gore of Homer, David's saga still shows the vigor and breakdown of the human body as people struggle with and against God's will. Now as we complete the book of Samuel and begin the book of Kings, the most vital man in the Tanach is shipwrecked by old age: "And King David had grown old, advanced in years, and they covered him with bedclothes, but he was not warm" (1 Kings 1:1). The Rabbis, ever seeking moral symmetry, recall David's snipping Saul's robe and say, "Whoever treats clothing without care in the end will derive no benefit from it" (Ber. 62b).

The book that is called Kings will begin with the death of the king remembered as the greatest of them all. This is not a grand, dramatic death. David will not climb a mountaintop as did Moses, to be gathered in God's arms. The story of David ends as it began, full of the sharp, sad reality of life.

David once tended his father's flock. His life changed in that moment, still fresh in our minds, when the young, bright-eyed boy is summoned by Saul to coax the king from melancholy. In an early unfinished play, Bertolt Brecht has the aged David wistfully remembering the days before Saul when he could be an idle shepherd. Once, long ago, before caught in the swirl of battles and betrayals, David lived quietly. In his dotage David returns to the indolence of youth. Many years before came the call that first changed his life, the command to find a lad to help cheer a gloomy king. Now reversing that call, David's servants ask leave to "seek out a young virgin" so that she can warm an aging one.

For most of his life David has been famously capable of finding his own women. In less reverential renderings, that is how David is sketched in later literature: The poet John Dryden will use David in his poem "Absalom and Ahitophel" as the model of an old philanderer, a foil to satirize Charles II. But during these final days David's vigor has ebbed. Others must provide his consort.

They seek a woman from throughout the kingdom, and Abishag is found and brought to the king. The text goes out of its way to tell us that she is beautiful but that the king does not become intimate with her—in the Bible's language, does not "know" her. With these few words the ineffectuality and even helplessness of David is made apparent. Even more than nature, monarchy abhors a vacuum. The scramble for a new king is about to begin.

Throughout David's career as king and parent, his inability to manage the passions and aspirations of his children has brought turmoil into his life and the life of all Israel. Clearly one of his sons will succeed him. As David's children jostle for position, he repeats the pattern of being unclear, or uninvolved, with his children. If he has given instructions, they are virtually unknown. Sidelined and diminished, how will he steer the future of the nation to which he gave his life?

Most scholars regard what follows as the culmination of one of the two major strands of narrative—kingship and succession—that make up the story of David. Both are presumed written to legitimate the Davidic line of kingship. Part of the succession story will take us beyond the confines of David's life into Solomon's reign, but most of the drama swirls around the king as his energy and life ebb away.

Novelists who have written on David seize on this moment of pathos and summation that characterize the end of a life. Alan Massie's *King David* imagines the aged king preoccupied with his predecessor Saul and his successor Solomon. Exhausted and reflective, David is puzzled by the course of his own life. Earlier in the novel, when Adonijah asks his father whether he understands himself, David answers, "No, does anyone?"

Almost all the novelists who seek to enter David's mind decide that as much as David may shun genuine introspection, one thing he is convinced of is that his will is a reflection of God's. They see David as a sort of Cromwell, devout in word and mostly so at heart, but also ruthless and brandishing piety like a scabbard hiding a blade. This may be too cynical, however, for we know that David often felt and suffered for his departure from God's wishes. The Psalms certainly reinforce this picture of self-doubt. The most powerful reimagining of David's story, Faulkner's *Absalom, Absalom*, includes multiple perspectives that frustrate any easy, single evaluation. Faulkner uses shifting voices and views that emphasize how ill-judged it is to fix on one quality in people to evaluate their lives. Like Faulkner's Sutpen, David sabotages his family and pays a dear price; but even though Faulkner's prose is far more interior (monologues, frequent incursions into people's thought processes) than anything the Bible has to offer, biblical narrative, with its deceptively simple surface, allows us to understand David deeply: He believes himself loved by God and chosen by God. Yet he also knows, given the tragedies of his life, that God's favor is never given without cost. Those costs undercut any temptation to self-righteousness. Novelists are drawn to David because the complexity of modern literature is well suited to this most intricately woven, colorful, and complicated portrait in the entire Bible.

Knowing the fullness of the burden of kingship in a way no one else can, David has nonetheless left the crucial matter of succession unassigned. Adonijah, whose mother was Haggith, is David's fourth-oldest son. He follows Amnon, who was killed by Absalom, Daniel (or Chileab), second-born, about whom nothing is said and who plays no real part in the story, and Absalom himself (listed in 1 Chron. 3:1). As the oldest surviving candidate, Adonijah is heir apparent to the throne.

Character is fate, said the Greeks, a lesson continually reinforced by the Bible. Rather than beginning with Adonijah's eventual fate, the story continues with his character: "And Adonijah son of Haggith was giving himself airs, saying, 'I shall be king'" (1 Kings 1:5).

We are tacitly invited to compare the behavior of Adonijah to his father, who appeared modest early in life. David was anointed by Samuel and acclaimed by the people, yet still did not promote himself as the present or future king. One need not trumpet the inevitable. The compulsion to do so reflects a vanity on the part of Adonijah, and a quick flip of the page to Proverbs (16:18) reminds us that pride goes before a fall. Adonijah rides in a chariot with an advance guard of fifty men, which is an exact copy of the early actions of Absalom. Like Absalom, Adonijah is called handsome. Perhaps Adonijah is seeking to appeal to those who still yearn for the rule of Absalom that never came to be. Political loyalties can die hard, and there were probably those who pined after Absalom and told their children stories of the greatness that briefly existed, in the manner of old communists saddened by the demise of the world in which they were young.

Part of the tragedy of Absalom was David's neglect and inability to set boundaries for his son. Having learned that lesson, we presume, David will now, even in his weakened state, see to it that Adonijah does not repeat the folly of the past. But people grow unevenly; some lessons we learn, while other flaws, constitutional in our characters, resist change. Perhaps as a result of his own guilt with Bathsheba, exacerbated by experiences with Amnon and Absalom, David has long been unable to discipline his children. Chaos engulfs his home. Now we are told of the strutting Adonijah: "And his father never caused him pain, saying, 'Why have you done this?'" (1 Kings 1:6). The word for "caused him pain"—"atsvo"—means "troubled him," or in the Septuagint reading, "restrained him." David never rebukes his son, never even asks him to justify himself. Adonijah has been so fecklessly indulged that his father did not bother to encourage self-examination.

Adonijah secures an important ally, Joab, whose position as commander of David's forces give his endorsement great weight. Adonijah is also assured of the loyalty of Abiathar, the priest who fled from Saul with David and stood by him during the revolt of Absalom. Adonijah throws a great feast and invites his kin, as well as the men of Judah. But we are also told whom Adonijah does not invite, which subtly informs us who was not supportive of his bid for the kingship: Nathan the prophet, the "warriors" (that is, David's elite guard), and his half-brother Solomon. As the other brothers were invited, battle lines have been drawn, and the plotting for succession between Adonijah and Solomon has begun.

Since David's adultery with Bathsheba and his subsequent confrontation with the prophet Nathan, we have heard nothing of those two. We know of no association between them.

Suddenly Nathan reappears and addresses Bathsheba. He warns her that her life is on the line because Adonijah has become king and David is unaware of the development. Our sense of David's distance from palace intrigue is reinforced. He is yet again blind to his son's plotting to capture the kingship. Speaking with Bathsheba, Nathan has a strategy:

> Go and get you to King David and say to him, "Has not my lord the king sworn to your servant, saying: Solomon your son shall be king after me, and he shall sit on my throne. And why has Adonijah become king? Look, while you are still speaking there, I shall come after you and fill in your words."
> (1 Kings 1:13–14)

Was this promise of David's to Bathsheba a memory or a fabrication on Nathan's part? The vow is not mentioned anywhere else in the story, nor are we given any more indication of its verity or falsehood. It does raise one intriguing possibility, however. Nathan's association with Bathsheba may go back much farther than we know. Perhaps the prophet knew Bathsheba or at least her family before she was taken by David. That may have been the catalyst for his intervention and censure of David in the first place. Jerusalem, all of Israel for that matter, was a small place indeed, and it would be no surprise if Nathan knew her. His outrage might have been the indignation not just of the prophet but of a family friend. We cannot know for sure, but whatever the original association, it is clear that the bond is now real and Nathan intends to strategize with Bathsheba to enthrone her son.

Bathsheba, so central to the drama of Israel's history, has thus far been recorded speaking two words, "I'm pregnant." She now proves herself as adept as the women who preceded her, such as Abigail and the wise woman of Tekoa, in moving David to the conclusion she desires.

Bathsheba enters the king's room where Abishag is ministering to David. Brushing past the woman who has youth but lacks history with David, Bathsheba reminds her husband (or informs him?) that he has promised that Solomon will one day sit on the throne. Then she tells David that his son Adonijah has already proclaimed himself king, is holding a feast, and has invited Joab and Abiathar but not Solomon.

Bathsheba tells him what he must surely know: that she and Solomon will be regarded as traitors if David dies and Adonijah becomes king. David has spent a lifetime watching the cut and thrust of palace politics. He understands Bathsheba's fear that she and Solomon will be sequestered at best, but more likely killed. In other words, David will be responsible for the death of the other child he fathered with Bathsheba, as he was responsible, through his sin, for the first. Whether David recalls or believes her claim that he promised the throne to Solomon we cannot know; he does not have time to evaluate it on its own merits, and perhaps it does not even matter to him. As Bathsheba is speaking, Nathan walks in and takes up the thread of the tale as Bathsheba discreetly retreats.

Nathan plays the moment masterfully. If David did swear to Bathsheba, it was presumably a private vow, not one to which Nathan would be privy, so he shifts the grounds of the discussion: "My lord the king, have you yourself said 'Adonijah shall be king after me and he shall sit on my throne'?" This he surely has not done and Nathan knows it. The prophet is reminding David of his son arrogantly asserting a right to the throne. Nathan confirms Bathsheba's report of Adonijah's feast and his audacious claim to kingship. Whether David made the promise to Solomon or not, he cannot help but be offended. Once again he is being usurped by his son, treated as though he is gone before leaving. Psalm 5 captures David's respect for God's standards of humility: "The arrogant cannot stand in Your presence, You detest all who do evil and doom those who speak lies" (Ps. 5:5–6).

As biblical scholar Baruch Halpern puts it, "David sprang, creaking, into action." He summons Bathsheba and swears by God that the promise he made to her (which he either remembers, believes he remembers, or pretends to remember) he will fulfill—to make Solomon king. Bathsheba responds with the appropriate, quixotic, and in the instance, paradoxical prayer, "May my lord king David live forever" (1 Kings 1:31).

Having been declared king multiple times, David knows how to anoint another one. The coronation ceremony had as much symbolism in ancient times as today, and in a contested succession, perhaps more. David summons Benaiah, now the head of David's guard since Joab switched to Adonijah's camp. He further summons his priest Zadok, who had wished to accompany David when he fled Jerusalem but was sent back with the ark. Along with Joab, David's former confederate the priest Abiathar is supporting Adonijah, whether aware or not of David's intentions to name Solomon his successor. Nathan will now superintend as the general Benaiah and priest Zadok watch Solomon mount David's own mule, as befits a new ruler of Israel. Solomon will ride down to the spring of Gihon, right outside the walls of Jerusalem, and there, to the sounding of the ram's horn, he will publicly be declared king. With a priest, a prophet, and a still living king inviting him to sit on his own throne, the act will be decisive.

The party planners do their work. "And all the people went up after him, and the people were playing flutes and making such revelry that the very earth split apart with their noise" (1 Kings 1:40). Word quickly spreads through Adonijah's camp that the ceremony is for Solomon and that David has blessed the Solomonic succession.

With his quick, sharp pen the author lets us know just how deep are the allegiances to Adonijah: "And all of Adonijah's invited guests trembled and rose up and each man went on his way" (1 Kings 1:49). We can imagine them filing out, giving Adonijah a quick pat of condolence on the back, wishing him nothing but the best.

Adonijah seeks the one possibility for refuge offered by the circumstances. He grasps the horns of the altar, an act which traditionally is thought to confer immunity from assault or punishment. Solomon, in an act reminiscent of the publicly largehearted side of his father, declares that if Adonijah proves decent, he will not be harmed—literally, not a hair of his will fall to the ground. But if he proves evil, decrees the new king, he will die.

Solomon's men come and take Adonijah from the altar, and he bows low before his brother Solomon. Solomon sends him, unharmed, to his house. No one can expect that it will end there, nor does it. For the idiom of no hair falling to the ground is familiar to us from David's plea on behalf of Absalom, and the echo of Absalom's fate hovers—a violent death at the hands of the king's men. If Solomon has learned anything from his father —and we shall see that he has—it is not to leave a rival, untouched, in place.

The first sentence of the first chapter of the first book of Kings reads, "King David was old." One chapter later, as the Rabbis point out, the opening sentence reads "David was dying." "King" David is old but just "David" is dying. When one is dying, he is neither king, nor doctor, nor priest, just a frail and fading man. What we see in David's final moments is his distilled character, as when a strong wind blows the leaves from a tree, leaving the trunk and branches visible. David is a combination of foresight, faith, and calculation, a man divided but decisive, confused about family but managing, in the end, to impose his will.

David begins with a peroration that many scholars believed was tacked on later to blunt the bloodthirstiness that follows. On his deathbed David admonishes his son to keep God's ways,

God's statutes and commands, so that he may prosper: "So that the Lord may fulfill His word that He spoke unto me, saying, 'If your sons keep their way to walk before Me in truth their whole heart and with their whole being, no man of yours will be cut off from the throne of Israel'" (1 Kings 2:4). That might have served as an apt final father-to-son farewell, but instead David proceeds to supply Solomon with a hit list.

He begins by reminding Solomon about Joab. Joab, who killed both Abner and Amasa (the leaders of Saul's and Absalom's armies, respectively), Joab who "shed the blood of war in peace." David does not mention Joab's execution of Absalom. He might consider it impolitic to remind Solomon at this moment of his love for another sibling. Instead, David simply instructs Solomon, in the Bible's idiom of violent death, not to let Joab's gray hairs go down to Sheol in peace.

David does not finish his litany of score-settling with Joab. He reminds Solomon of the loyalty of the sons of Barzillai—Solomon should keep faith with them—and the treachery of Shimei, who cursed him as he ran from Absalom. He tells Solomon that he, David, promised not to hurt Shimei. However: "Do not hold him guiltless, for you are a wise man, and you will know what you should do to him, and bring his gray head down in blood to Sheol" (1 Kings 2:9).

Professor Gene Veith Jr. comments that "the story of David suggests the paradox that all evil must be punished, but it is heroic to refrain from punishing." David has held back. Now in his final moments he seeks revenge, or what he perceives to be justice. The man who was so forceful in life will prove posthumously fierce as well.

David's last words are in the interest of his own vengefulness, of course, which like that of *The Godfather*'s Don Corleone (scenes of which draw from David), reaches from beyond the grave. These vindictive instructions are also offered for Solomon's benefit. This son has not yet been in the rough-and-tumble of kingly politics. Though Solomon will prove adept, David wishes to identify the key adversaries. Shimei, representative of the North, might still be able to rouse a rebellion. And Joab is a dangerous man. David's final words to his son, violent though they may be, could also be seen as a paternal embrace, anticipating Leonard Cohen's magnificent musical riff on David, *Hallelujah:* "But all I've ever learned from love / Was how to shoot somebody who outdrew ya."

The postscript consists of a son requesting his father's consort for himself. Adonijah approaches Bathsheba to ask whether he might be given Abishag, the concubine who has lain beside David in the king's last days. This is a move so stunningly tone-deaf that it led the biblical scholar Frank Cross to say that if Adonijah indeed did it, he deserved to be executed for sheer stupidity. To take the king's mistress is a clear bid for royal status. Why do something so transparently treacherous? Adonijah may have been responsible for placing Abishag with David in the first place. One speculation is that he selected her to see whether his father was impotent, and upon discovering that he was, declared himself king. Now he wishes to "reclaim" her. But why does he approach Bathsheba, Solomon's mother, to press his request? She is the least likely to look upon any desire of Adonijah's with a generous eye. The entire story is baffling, but its outcome is predictable, so predictable as to lead to speculation that it was an invention to create a pretext. Solomon orders his inept and threatening half-brother killed by Benaiah. In the manner of his father, one more rival down.

Solomon learns the lessons of strategic lenience as well. The priest Abiathar was kind to David but cast his lot with Adonijah. Solomon, while banishing him, leaves him unharmed. Killing a priest might raise the uncomfortable specter of one of the sins for which Saul was stripped of kingship, the slaughter of the priests of Nob. Joab, on the other hand, who enjoys no such sacerdotal immunity, realizes from long experience what awaits him and runs to the altar and grabs the horns. When Benaiah tries to coax him out in Solomon's name, Joab refuses, clinging to the horns of the altar for dear life, saying "No, for here I shall die" (1 Kings 2:30).

When Joab's words are reported to Solomon, he reveals that the icy blood of his father runs in his veins as well, recalling the murders of Abner and Amasa, and telling Benaiah, "Do as he has spoken, and stab him and bury him, and you shall take away the blood that Joab shed for no cause, from me and from my father's house" (1 Kings 2:31). Benaiah strikes him down.

In the final act of the David story, before Solomon lives his own tale, Solomon puts Shimei under house arrest, warning him that if he leaves the confines of Jerusalem, over the Wadi Kidron which separates his home from his native village of Bahurim, he will die. For two years Shimei carefully observes the border. Then he is told that two of his slaves have run away to Gath, the Philistine capital. He will have to violate the restriction to reclaim his property across the border. Shimei goes to recapture the slaves. Solomon's message is vintage David:

> "Did I not make you swear by the Lord and warn you, saying, 'The day you go out and move about hither and yon, you must surely know that you are doomed to die? . . . You yourself know all the evil, which your own heart knows, that you did to David my father, and the Lord has brought back your evil on your own head. But King Solomon shall be blessed and the throne of David shall be unshaken before the Lord forevermore.'" And the king charged Benaiah son of Jeohaiada, and he went out and stabbed him, and he died. (1 Kings 2:44–46)

As David once fled from Saul to Gath, so Shimei, the Saul sympathizer who cursed David, goes to Gath, and David's son executes him for this flight. The narrative circle of Saul and David is closed.

9

The Once and Future King

THE LINEAGE of the Messiah in Judaism is distinguished by its improbability: It comes through the quasi-incest of Judah (sex with his daughter-in-law), a convert from a people with whom Israel fought (Ruth from Moab), and adultery (David and Bathsheba). The decisive figure in this messianic lineage is David. He is also the most unlikely ancestor of all. Even in modern Israel, David remains controversial. Shimon Peres, responding to a religious member of the Knesset, said, "I recognize the Torah of Moses our teacher and not the Torah of David our patriarch. . . . Not everything King David did on land, or on roofs, appears to me to be Judaism." In Peres's sentence "on land" refers to conquest, "on roofs" to David's adultery with Bathsheba. Israel's president could say openly what many others had felt: David was no role model. The seventeenth-century Enlightenment savant Pierre Bayle had to withdraw his article on David from his *Dictionary* because his condemna-

tion of David for cruelties and betrayals was more severe than
the age-old (and more acceptable) condemnation of the sin of
adultery. David, wrote Bayle, "sacrificed justice to utility."

Yet despite myriad flaws, David captures the imagination
even more than Moses. In Marc Chagall's contrasting portraits,
Moses holds the stone tablets of the law and David carries a
harp. David is more human, flawed, artistic, approachable. Joseph Heller's David writes, in *God Knows*, that his story is the
best in the Bible: "I've got the poetry and passion, savage violence and the plain raw civilizing grief of human heartbreak."

For all that David may appeal to the love of an epic yarn,
Peres's point is one that echoes through the ages. What is it
about David that makes him the one to whom God bestows an
eternal promise? He is such a contradictory personality that
even the ancient rabbis confessed, "We are unable to make
sense of David's character" (PDRK 27:3).

David's predecessor Saul is rejected by God in favor of
David. The Protestant theologian Dietrich Bonhoeffer, com-
paring Saul's slaughter of the priests of Nob to David's adultery
with Bathsheba, says that God more readily forgives sins of weakness than sins of strength. Rabbenu Tam, the medieval Talmud-
ist, argues that David's transgression was unrelated to his responsibilities as king, whereas Saul's failure to kill the Philistine
king Agag was a sin affecting statecraft. One medieval Jewish
philosopher, Joseph Albo, makes a kindred claim, arguing that
God weighed whether the infraction showed an inability to
carry out royal responsibilities: Saul's did and David's did not.

Still, there remains something forced about the responses.
The post facto answer is that the Bible is written to justify what
already exists. Kings from the line of David had court scribes
who shaped and molded the biblical tale to solidify their legacy
and position of power. We are entitled nonetheless to wonder
how this one man cast so great a shadow over the subsequent
history of the kingship of Israel. There is a story about the

Chofetz Chaim, the renowned rabbi of the nineteenth century, who was summoned as a character witness before a secular court. In order to illustrate the rabbi's eminence to the judge, the lawyer told tales of his learning and piety. When the judge questioned the veracity of the stories, the lawyer replied that he could not vouch for the literal truth of the tales but one thing he did know: "Your honor, they don't tell stories like that about you and me." Even if the author smoothed some stories and re-shaped others, there is something about David that gives rise to images of the wild, galvanizing figure who is a giant of the ages.

One of David's most distinguishing features was the sin he avoided: idolatry. Unlike many of his successors, not once in the entire David narrative does he worship idols or false gods. Apart from his confiscation of the enemy's idols after a conquest (2, 5:21), the only mention of idolatry is when Michal places a statue in the bed to cover for David's absence, permitting him to escape from Saul.

Not only is David free from the stain of idolatry, his relationship with God is steady and assured throughout the story. A staunch believer and a worshiper, David prays, offers thanks, and most important, hopes to build the Temple. His being credited with the Psalms solidifies the traditional depiction of David as the most devotional figure in the Bible. "I have set the Lord before me always" (Ps. 16:8). Typical of the interplay between the Psalms and rabbinic readings of David is Psalm 119:62: "I arise at midnight to praise you." The Rabbis asked how he woke at midnight. They imagined that he hung his harp above his bed, and God sent a nightly breeze, vibrating the strings of the instrument. Roused from sleep by music, David would praise God in the dark of night. The Talmud extends this theme in another passage insisting that David is the one chosen to say the Grace after meals in the heavenly world (Pesachim, 119b).

God is not always pleased with his servant's actions, to say the least. Still, throughout his journey, David, though sinful and rebuked, is never faithless. His failures do not make him doubt —or reject—God; rather, they intensify his devotion. Ben Sira writes that David loved his Creator and God took away his sin.

David is the king who founded a capital, subdued the Philistines, united North and South, proposed the Temple, and established a dynasty. The ancient historian Josephus praises him for seeking to quell civil dissent, a rupture that beset the Jewish people in Josephus's own time. All of these considerations play a role in the elevation of David to the status of ancestor of the Messiah.

In the Bible, the qualities of the Messiah are outlined very sketchily. We are told that "a shoot will come up from the stump of Jesse" (Is. 11:1), but his exact nature and activities are cloaked in metaphor. Since there are no supernatural qualities attributed to the Messiah in the Bible, in some deep way the Messiah is neither a godlike figure nor a simple human being, but a summation and culmination of human experience.

David is everything. Conventional religion has a regrettable tendency to do surgery on the human soul, leaving only the exalted parts. But readers of the Bible find that the original source is more realistic. The Bible is filled with flawed human beings and fraught situations against the backdrop of charged sanctity. The entire book is indeed, in Leonard Cohen's words, "a broken hallelujah." The tensions in families, the price of ambition, the hypocrisies that attend piety, the nobility and savagery of human beings—all are on colorful display in the pages of the Hebrew Bible. Such a book could not propose a candidate to represent the summation of human experience to whom these passions were alien. And there is no character who begins to approach David for the plentitude of human expression and emotion.

David fits as the ancestor of the Messiah precisely because of his weaknesses, his transgressions, his artifice, his divided heart.

He is great because of his complexity, not in spite of it. David is a man of contradictions, noble and base, lyrical and brutal, all of which coexist in a quieter state in each human breast. We see ourselves in this man, and we see this man in ourselves. The Tanach goes even farther than showing David as the archetype of every human being; he has in him a spark of the divine: When dismissing Saul, Samuel says to the fallen king: "But now your kingdom shall not stand. The Lord has already sought out for Himself a man after his own heart" (1, 13:14).

After God's own heart: David in character is like God in action. The inexplicable amalgam of good and evil is filtered through human hearts that embrace the totality of God's world, not timid like Saul but daring, volatile, dangerous, and epic like David. Isaiah says that God "makes peace and creates evil" (Is. 45:7). In other words all things have their source in God. David stands like Lear on the heath, an epitome of earthly experience, raging, beset, the one who feels most deeply, the one who has God's heart. Perhaps David is the forerunner of the Messiah because this is the man who enacts what God wishes—in his sinfulness and sublimity, he is the most human of us all.

SUGGESTED READING

There are endless books and articles about David, many of them both thoughtful and helpful. In English, begin by reading the books of 1 and 2 Samuel in a good translation. I suggest Robert Alter's *The David Story* (whose translation I have used in this book), Everett Fox's *Give Us a King!*, or the New JPS translation in *Tanakh*. For those who want a readable walk through David's life, Jonathan Kirsch is an able guide in his *King David: The Real Life of the Man Who Ruled Israel*, and Robert Pinsky has written a short, poetic book entitled *The Life of David*.

To dig a bit deeper, you can turn to the "prosecutors": scholars who take a dark view of David. Steven McKenzie, in *King David: A Biography*, marshals evidence and argument to indict David for a wide range of crimes. The most comprehensive and intricate study is Baruch Halpern, *David's Secret Demons: Messiah, Murderer, Traitor, King*. As the title implies, it too is not an entirely flattering portrait. Suggestive and interesting takes on David, with a kinder view of his personality, are found in Marti Steussy's *David: Biblical*

Portraits of Power and Paul Borgman, *David, Saul, and God.* Jacob Wright, in *King David and His Reign Revisited*, seeks to untangle the sources and motivations of the stories.

This book was enriched by works by such renowned modern scholars as David Gunn, Walter Brueggemann, Joel Rosenberg, Jon Levenson, Robert Polzin, P. Kyle McCarter Jr., and many other contributors to the landscape of David's modern image. Their books are well worth seeking for the interested student. Because of the prominence of David's legacy in Judaism, not only the Talmud and Midrash but virtually all classical and contemporary Jewish commentators, from Rashi in medieval times to Hasidic writers and modern Israeli scholars, explore David's character and accomplishments, though much of this material is available only in Hebrew. Among the traditional voices, I found Abravanel the most suggestive, although Rabbi David Kimchi and Ralbag, who wrote extensively on Samuel, offer invaluable insights as well. The most skillful of the many novels imagining David's life is Stefan Heym, *The King David Report.*

ACKNOWLEDGMENTS

Thanks to Professor Steven Zipperstein, who asked if I would take on this fascinating project and, along with Anita Shapira, Ileene Smith, and Dan Heaton, shepherded it through to completion. I first studied David's story in the book of Samuel with my dear friend Dr. Robert Wexler, whose classes sparked a passion for Tanach in a generation of students. Eileen Wolpe and Abby Pogrebin each gave the book a careful, red-penciled reading, from which it benefited greatly. Nancy Josephson envisioned the larger possibilities of the David story from the first word; thanks to her and to the terrific David Black. Menachem Butler provided some intriguing scholarly leads, as did Leon Wieseltier, and the library at American Jewish University allowed me to track them down. Staff and congregants at Sinai Temple are ever supportive and encouraging about the byways and interests of their rabbi, and I am grateful. Each Thursday morning our synagogue Torah class gathers to study David; their insights and questions proved both provocative and helpful. Thanks to my wonderful assistant, Rebecca Davenport, my exemplary colleagues Rabbis Nicole Guzik and Jason Fruithandler, Cantor Marcus Feldman, Ralph Resnick, and Howard Lesner, as well as Mike Karz, Esther Jonas-Maertin, Danielle Berrin, Jonathan Segal, Kirk Douglas, and Niija Kuykendall. My daughter Samara's wry, loving skepticism, along with her buoyant spirit, trails each sentence. Rabbi Gerald Wolpe, my father of blessed memory, named me David after the uncle who helped raise him when his own father died. To my father and mother, as well as the namesake uncle I never knew, more gratitude and love than I can express.

INDEX

JEWISH LIVES is a major series of interpretive
biography designed to illuminate the imprint of Jewish
figures upon literature, religion, philosophy, politics, cultural
and economic life, and the arts and sciences. Subjects are
paired with authors to elicit lively, deeply informed books that
explore the range and depth of Jewish experience
from antiquity through the present.

Jewish Lives is a partnership of Yale University Press
and the Leon D. Black Foundation.

Ileene Smith is editorial director. Anita Shapira and
Steven J. Zipperstein are series editors.